NRC

NRC

D1099954

NO DEALS

An Addict's Journey to Freedom

JACKIE BURKE

WITH BRENDA WOODS

POOLBEG

Published 2007
by Poolbeg Press Ltd
123 Grange Hill, Baldoyle
Dublin 13, Ireland
E-mail: poolbeg@poolbeg.com
www.poolbeg.com

1 3 5 7 9 10 8 6 4 2

A catalogue record for this book is available from the British Library.

ISBN 978-1-84223-305-4

Typeset by Patricia Hope in Sabon 11.5/15
Litografia Rosés, S.A., Spain

www.poolbeg.com

About the authors

Jackie Burke lives in Lisburn, County Antrim with his wife and three children. Having spent much of his adult life as a registered drug addict he is now a Christian and travels around Ireland to schools and colleges with his message of hope. He can be contacted at hilary877@msn.com

Brenda Woods is a journalist. She works as a feature writer with *The Evening Herald* and is Editor of *GATE* magazine for young people. Brenda also freelances for various publications around the country. She is married and lives in Dundalk, County Louth, with her husband and two children.

Acknowledgements

From Jackie:

Special thanks to my wife Hilary – my love, my best friend
. . . and my fiercest critic! I am eternally grateful to you for
all your hard work and the inspiration behind the title,
No Deals. For Matthew, Rachel and Jonathan, for your
laughter, love and happy hearts. Thanks also to Raymond
and Joan, for all your support and "fresh horses". And
thanks to Hilary's family for all their support and
understanding.

Brenda, I am eternally grateful to you for your patience,
humour and skill. Thanks also to Ned and Peter, fellow
travellers and mavericks; to Roger, for your friendship
and for opening the door to that first classroom; and to
Davina for friendship, fellowship and Sunday lunches!

Thanks to all at Poolbeg Press, but especially to Brian for
your expertise and Kieran for taking that chance on me.

From Brenda:

A very big thank you to my husband Eddie, and to my
two children, Áoise and Edward. You are always there

supporting and loving. I could not have done this without you. Love you all.

Thanks also to mum and dad and to the Finegan family for everything. Gerry and Kathleen, thank you for leading me to Jackie; and thanks also to Suzanne and Una. Indirectly thanks to Dave Diebold at *The Evening Herald* for letting real-life heroes shine in the spotlight. Thanks also to Stephen Rae.

A special thank you to Brian Langan at Poolbeg Press, who used his talents and real understanding to bring everything together. Kieran Devlin and Paula Campbell, thank you so much for helping "the baby" to take its first steps! Please God it will grow into a well-behaved child! The support you have given me to realise this memoir has been sincerely appreciated.

To the Burke family for opening their lives to me. Hilary, thank you for your patience and dedication to the book. I would like to say a word of thanks also to Jackie's mother Susan. This was an important story to tell, and I thank you for being there and for your strength. Finally, Jackie: thank you so much for sharing your life story not only with me but with others and for being selfless and showing what true humanity is all about. It has been a privilege.

Note: The names of many people whose lives are touched on in this memoir have been changed to protect their anonymity.

For Mum – Jackie

For Eddie, Áoise and Edward – Brenda

Prologue

I'm looking for a good night's sleep. God? Don't talk to me about God! If God's there, he's deaf. I've no time for God. It's four o'clock in the morning, and I wake up with this prayer coming out of my mouth: "Father, Father, please, please don't let me die like this." What's going on? I try to get out of bed, sit down, but my legs buckle beneath me and I hit the floor.

It's called barbiturate poisoning. It starts down at your feet; it lifts up through your whole body as it travels towards your heart. It can kill you in a matter of hours. I know what I need to do here; I need to get into the Lagan Valley Hospital, get a saline drip into me, and get my whole system cleaned out. I need to do it pretty quickly. I know this because I've taken overdoses in the past, some of them deliberate. I know the problem, and I know the solution.

But I know something else. There is someone in that room with me, and He's more real to me than you are now reading this.

I crawl into the living room, get up and lie down on the sofa. Pages of my memory are turning and He's saying: "Jackie, you've tried everything else, would you not try me? Jackie, you've done that now, would you not come to me?"

Chapter 1

The first thing I have to tell you about myself is what I am not. I am not one of those boys who you've seen on *Oprah, Ricki Lake* or *Jeremy Kyle.* I didn't take drugs because my mum didn't like me. I didn't take drugs because my dad beat me. I didn't even take drugs because my auntie fancied me! I didn't take drugs for any of these reasons. I took drugs because it was all an adventure and an experiment that got out of control. At least, that's why I thought I took drugs.

Why is it that only we humans take drink and drugs? You don't see lions going down the street drunk or monkeys swaying from the trees smoking dope. So why do we human beings have this need to get drunk and stoned? I think we do it to make ourselves feel happier. But why are we unhappy to begin with?

Well, they put me in prison on four occasions; they thought they could scare me off drugs. It didn't work.

They put me in psychiatric hospitals on seven occasions; they were going to cure me of my drug habit. Didn't work.

Why didn't it work? Why couldn't the police and the prison officers scare me off drugs? Why couldn't the doctors, the psychiatrists and the psychologists cure me of them? I think they were missing one vital point: why was I taking drink and drugs in the first place? What was the real reason behind it?

This is the only way I can explain it. Imagine yourself sitting at home. It's half past eleven at night, you are in your living room reading this. There's one difference: you are on your own. Your husband, wife, children, mum, dad, your brothers, or sisters, whoever you happen to live with, they have all been called away on some urgent business. They couldn't bring you with them, so you get this book out to pass the time. Remember, you've no friends around to keep your image up for you. You know that image. It is the one you show people, the one that says, "This is who I am." But you know inside it is not really the whole story. It's just you in the empty house.

You go to bed. Nothing is disturbing you. You start to relax and fall asleep. But in the early hours of the morning, for no reason at all, you suddenly wake up. In that moment, just for a split second, you feel a bit frightened. You don't know why, but a thought, a feeling, it's hard to describe, just comes into your head. It's only there and it's gone, and the thought is this: *Is this it, is this all there is?* You begin to think: *I'll go to school, get a certificate, get a job, find somebody I love, get married, have a couple of kids, and then I die? And while I'm doing all this, everybody around me, they are all going to die too? My mum and dad, my brothers, my sisters, my friends? This house is going to be empty one day? There won't ever be a memory of me and my family having lived here? Is that the whole story – the whole purpose of life?*

I'm sure you might not have had that exact experience, but having spoken to 25,000 teenagers last year alone, I can assure you, no one has walked up to me after my talk, looked me in the eyes and said: "Jackie, I've never had a moment like that – that for no reason I simply felt that small." Do you see your image of yourself? It's not worth that. You are that small size in a big universe that is revolving around you. Do you see that when a thought like that hits you, it can make you feel very empty inside? That emptiness: that is the real reason why we take drink and drugs.

I tried to drown my emptiness out through alcohol. I tried to bury my loneliness with pills. I tried to inject my insecurity away. But not even heroin, the strongest drug on God's green earth, can keep that emptiness down. Do you know why? That emptiness is God-shaped, and only God can fill it. I didn't find that out for a long time.

Chapter 2

I was born in 1953. My mum's name is Susan; my dad's name was John. My oldest brother was Tom or Thomas, and my other brother is Raymond. My two older brothers also went by the nicknames of "Amos", because there was a television programme on at the time called *Burke's Law* with a character called Amos Burke in it. To this day Raymond still gets called Amos.

As a kid, everything went right for me, in my home life and in my education. I had all the right support mechanisms. I had a father who, very unusually for that period of time, took delight in communicating and sharing life with his sons. We lived and spent our childhood in Tonagh Estate in Lisburn, in a very good environment. It was full of young families, so there were always gangs of young people roaming the streets, playing cowboys and Indians. It was ideal. Tonagh Estate got the nickname, as the Troubles began, of Vatican City, because the estate was made up of mixed religions, but it was mostly Catholic.

Dad was originally from Wicklow, where he had grown up with a father who was a great disciplinarian. Don't get me wrong; my granddad Burke was good to his sons and daughters. But as soon as they were of age, they were marched off to join the RAF or the British Army. Granddad Burke's attitude was, "Get them out and get them to see the world." I think that love sometimes took second place in his life. My dad made a promise when my mum was pregnant with Tom; he said to her, "You can do whatever you see fit with our children, but never expect me to raise my hand to them, because I just couldn't." Through all the years of us kids provoking him, dad kept his word and he never raised his hand. He just had this look – a look that would say "will ye quit" – and most of the time that did the trick.

Unusually for a man who had grown up in a rural part of Ireland, as Wicklow was then, he had spent years in the army, with no home to speak of. But when he met my mother, and he fell in love, and when we came along, his delight was tangible. My contemporaries would talk about their dad in a distant way, and I thought everybody had a dad like mine – somebody who would sit down and chat with you. I don't want to make it sound too good to be true, but it was very definitely an ideal upbringing. No sacrifice was too great for them, and that was to remain the case, not just in my childhood, but as I grew up and as I got involved in drugs. Nothing was ever too great a step for them. I grew up believing everybody had parents like mine.

I had no possible reason in my home life to suggest I would get involved in drink and drugs.

My dad met my mum while he was in the army. He had been stationed in Tiefield Barracks in Belfast during the war and was friends with a guy called Jim McKeown. Jim used to sing the praises of this girl back in Lisburn whom he had hoped, one day, to come back and propose to. As the war progressed, Jim got stationed out in Borneo and died. So my dad, stationed where he was, decided it would be a nice gesture to go over to visit Jim's parents, and to say what good friends they had been and how he had thought a lot of Jim. He found out where the McKeown family lived in Lisburn. He put on his big grey overcoat one night and marched off. As he got nearer to the street where Jim lived, he saw two girls walking towards him. One of them was Susan Totten – my mum. The other was her friend. My dad introduced himself and asked them for directions to Barrack Street where Jim had lived. My mum identified right away who this John Burke character was and that made a strong connection between the two of them. Of course, my dad, never one to miss an opportunity, asked the girls where they were going that night. They told him they were going to the dance at the local British Legion Hall, where all the British army headed to. He asked if they would mind if he were to accompany them. They agreed. My dad went to see Jim's parents and the girls went on their way. My dad would swear that when he went into that British Legion Hall later on, he took just one look at my mum, asked her for a dance, and fell in love.

Of course my dad was a clever man in many ways; he knew how to engineer a situation to his advantage. After all, he did go through the war without one shot ever being fired at him and, because of his astuteness and his ability, he had been made Sergeant. So my dad got his time in the army extended to Lisburn so he could spend the rest of the year there. Most nights he spent visiting my mum and taking her out. At the end of the year, dad proposed and my mum said yes. He then applied and got a further extension of time in Lisburn, because my mum's mother was very ill and was near death. My granny had said to mum to get married and do it quickly. So they got married and, about a month or so later, my granny died.

While the war still continued to rage, my mum recalled that, for the next four years, she had the greatest romance in the world. The army would send my dad away to Wales for a few months at a time to train troops for the front lines. When he would be due home on leave, my mum would hurry to the train station and wait eagerly for him on the platform. The reunions would be very eventful and then the romance would begin all over again for them.

My dad always included me in everything that was going on. My earliest memory is of him lifting me out of bed in the dark night to bring me downstairs to show me something magical. It was just like a visit from Santa. I was so excited. He told me he had brought something wonderful home and when he opened the door of the living-room, there it was – our first ever television set. It was throwing black and white shapes out across the carpet floor, and it seemed to me like something from another world. I just stared at it for a few seconds, while above my head I listened to my parents chatting excitedly about it, and watched the brothers darting across and in front of the screen.

There were plenty more magical times like that. Dad would often take us boys off on an adventure, and we would have to get lots of supplies together before we could set out. Mum would be working feverishly at the kitchen table, making up lots of bread and jam sandwiches and wrapping them into little paper bundles for us, and telling us all to mind ourselves and to stick close to dad. There we were – dad, Tom, Raymond and myself – all set for our big day out, smiling with innocence, wondering where we could possibly end up. The adventure would usually begin with us walking over the field near our home, to a place called The Sandies – because there was so much sand in the little clearways. To us, this was like visiting another country.

Dad would be in charge and we would walk around the trees and shrubs until we came to a place where we could set up our little camp. Tom, being the eldest, was told to gather large stones. Off he'd go picking up this stone and that, carrying them back, his arms full of all shapes and sizes. It was then up to him to put them into a circle on the ground. Raymond had his own little task – to collect wood for the fire. Being the youngest, I had the easiest of the jobs and my mission was to gather little bushes and dry twigs for the base of the fire. "All set now," dad would say, and just like the cowboys we had seen on the television, dad would slowly build a little fire and set light to it. We would all sit around the little glowing flames. Dad then would produce a large tin can, usually scrounged from mum's larder. He would fill it with water from his flask, this was suspended across the fire and the tea leaves were added when it came to the boil. To this day, I have never tasted tea so rich or sandwiches so sweet. As we men sat around the fire, dad would talk to us about everything that interested us. Sometimes we would get him to tell us tales of World War II. He never made himself out to be a hero of these stories, and he preferred to make us laugh as he related some of the more silly characters he met while in action.

Often sitting around our little camp fire, dad would talk to us about mum. He told us how much of a lady she was and instilled in us how important she was. Whenever we went out as a whole family, as soon as we reached home, dad would automatically put the key in the lock of the front door, and then step back. We fellas all knew to stand back until mum entered the house first. We were always told that manners were free, but vitally important.

I was always asking mum and dad for a dog. My brothers and I had a habit of bringing stray ones in from the street on a regular basis. My poor dad would wash and feed them but within a day or two they would disappear. Gradually dad warmed to the idea of getting a dog for me. It happened one Friday night. Every Friday after work dad brought us home some sweets; they'd be hiding in different pockets of his coat. It was our job to riffle these pockets when he came through the door. So when he arrived, I was first to plunge my hand into the right pocket of his great big raincoat – where you were always guaranteed the best sweets. My two brothers shared the left pocket. But this evening as we walked away, dad said: "Haven't you forgotten something, Jackie?" There, poking his little head out from the inside of the coat, was the cutest little black Labrador cross puppy.

We named him Bronco after a cowboy my brothers saw in a film. That dog became so wise and he never left my side. If I was out playing and mum wanted me to come home, she would say to Bronco, "Go find Jackie." Wherever I was playing, the dog would find me, stand there looking up at me and bark; and I would know it was time to go home.

Dad would take us the odd time to Belfast for bigger adventures. One time dad and I had been in Belfast having a great day out when it started to rain and we were in a rush to catch the train home. All along the streets of this city, everything looked so big to me. Snuggled into the flap of his raincoat, on that very wet, windy day, I kept asking him questions: "What is that?" "Who lives there?" I was mesmerised by the enormity, the grandeur of it all. Then I said, "Dad, you don't mind me asking, do you?" And right there, in the middle of Great Victoria Street, he got down on one knee to bring his face close to mine and said, "Son, never stop asking questions. That is how we learn." I felt my dad was a hero.

Our summers were fantastic. Every year the whole family would pack up and get the train to Dublin to go and stay with our relations in Wicklow. The train journey down was fascinating. We would look out the window and watch all the unfamiliar places whizzing by, and read the names of unknown places. When we would get into Connolly Station, dad's brother Robert would meet us and pack us all into the car to drive to Wicklow. There, standing at the door of the big farmhouse, would be Granny Burke. We would rush to her open arms, where we all got the greatest hugs before she would bundle us into the old kitchen and feed us more food than any horse could eat.

Those holidays were heaven-sent. One day we would be swimming in the lakes; the next, heading out with our uncle on his little speedboat, no less. It was a time of laughter, exploring new things, making new friends and enjoying the company of our cousins.

Chapter 3

I was brought up in a good home where my parents loved each other and that love was filtered down very much into our upbringing. I was in an even better position than my brothers; being the youngest I was in many ways spoilt rotten.

My two older brothers were typical Northern Ireland brothers. They would go out and fight your battles for you, then take you home and give you a good dressing down for getting into trouble in the first place. We were a tight loving family. We were not rich, but neither were we poor. We lived in a typical three-bedroom house. My two brothers shared one bedroom and I had my own room. My mother would leave the bedroom doors wide open each night and the landing light was left on. That way nobody would ever be afraid of the dark.

There was another reason for leaving the doors open, though. When we all got undressed and into bed, my mum would say, "Boys, time to pray", and we would say the "Our Father" together. Mum had a lovely ending to that prayer. She would add: ". . . and keep us all in our right senses". I don't know why those particular words were always on my mother's lips. It seemed that she always believed you could battle ill health, but that losing your mind would be an awful thing. As it turned out, she was right. For me, losing my mind through drugs and drink would be a nightmare. Despite all the love I had, I ended up taking drugs. What went wrong?

There was one thing that did depress me growing up, and that was Sundays. I hated them. Every Sunday my mum and dad would dress myself and the brothers up like dogs' dinners and march us off to the local Church of Ireland church. I didn't disrespect the preachers there, but I grew up with the attitude that, if God was out there, He was probably on the third cloud to the left. We would read about Him on a Sunday, but I always thought: *I've to get on with real life. God? He's nothing to do with real life.*

Don't get me wrong, though; I never had a problem *believing* in God. Occasionally, I would get something out of going to church. I remember going to Sunday School at an early age, and hearing about a prophet from the Old Testament who held a woollen fleece before God and said, "If you want me to do something, God, wet the whole side of the fleece." The story goes that, in the morning, the fleece was wet; the prophet then asked God to dry it and He did. So I thought this same tactic was going to pay off for me. It was coming up to the time of my 11-plus exams, and I made one of those bargaining prayers. I asked Our Lord if he could do the same sort of thing that he had done for that prophet, but in this case make me pass my exams, and then I would do my best to try to be a good person. As it turned out, I did do the exam and I did pass. I went on to Lisburn Technical College at the age of eleven.

The system there would take you through until the age of sixteen when you would do your O Levels, then on to the A Levels and then hopefully, university. In the first few years at school I did very well. I wasn't at the top of the class but I was far from the bottom. I loved English and English literature in particular. I made friends easily. There was a bunch of us and we called ourselves The Magnificent Seven. We were the tall, big guys in the school. We thought we were tough, that we could defend ourselves from any attacks, real or imaginary.

We started doing what a lot of other young people were doing at the time – smoking cigarettes. Looking back, I feel that simple step was the start of something, because we now know that the majority of people who smoke do go on to other drugs, mostly alcohol. It breaks down the barrier that prevents you doing something unnatural to your body. So, I smoked my first cigarette.

Then I got drunk for the first time. My first drink happened because I was hanging around with older guys from outside school, both Catholic and Protestant. I had two close friends in particular, Martin and Terry, who were a good two or three years older than me. Because I was tall for my age, I could get away with a lot more than the younger boys. I was also learning so much about life from my two older brothers and from their friends. I thought I was very mature, way beyond my thirteen years of age. But of course I wasn't.

My older friends had a guy in his twenties they called a runner. He would go into the off-licence and buy all the drink. For my first time, I got some pocket money, paid this guy for a half bottle of wine. I drank it and I felt absolutely free. That was my first drink. I suppose the excitement, the adrenalin rush of doing this amazing new thing was the best part of the buzz, because I didn't really enjoy getting drunk much. I was falling about the place, I didn't have control, and I wondered why I'd done it.

Of course at that age I was caught coming home drunk and my parents grounded me many times. But the next step into my progression with alcohol was six months down the line, when I learned the different ways I could get a hit from the bottle without ever going over the top. This meant I was reasonably together coming home to my parents. I picked these tricks up on the streets from the other kids. My drinking became my weekend thing, every weekend. A gang of us used to drink on the streets away from the estate. We would go into a row of condemned houses so we could have some privacy and not get caught. There could be as many as twenty or thirty of us, all together inside, drinking and smoking away.

Even though drinking cheap wine and beer dominated my weekend, the connection with God that lay in my upbringing kept pulling me a little in the other direction. Martin, Terry and I were members of the youth club, so I felt I was living a double life in some ways. We would spend most of the weekend afternoons off the side streets, drinking bottles of wine, and then we would try to sober up and go to the Church youth club for a dance that evening.

We had looked on our Confirmation as being our final connection with the Church of Ireland. Once we had got that over and finished with, we thought our parents would eventually get off our backs. We were attending Confirmation classes during the day and we would be boozing at the weekend. No wonder I always felt God was always "somebody out there", somebody I could never really get close to. My attitude was to change, though.

Chapter 4

By the age of fourteen, two influences came into my life that were to pull me in different directions. The first was to do with the "Holy Rollers" as we called them. They were the new breed of cleric. One day this young cleric arrived at our church. He was from Dun Laoghaire and his name was Dave Burnel. Now Dave was a bit different – Dave had long hair. Nowadays it's no big thing, but when I was fourteen, and I saw this guy, I thought, *He's one of us!*

And that was the second big influence that came into my life: the hippies had arrived! This was a big thing. I grew my hair long. I got my beads and my belts and daisy chains, and off I went to change the world with some mates.

What I did at this point in my life is what a lot of people do who have a sort of sneaking respect for religion, but don't want to get too involved in it, in case it might take over their lives or frighten them. I made a deal with it. I had read somewhere in the Bible that it said, "God is love". So, thinking I was really clever, I told myself that that would do me. I went down to see Dave. I told him, "Me and Big G, we're close." Dave was confused. I told him what it said in the Bible and that, because I was a hippy and believed in peace and love, it had to be all right with God if I was a hippy. Dave dismissed me and told me I didn't know the first thing about this love business. I was adamant. He told me to take the Bible and go off and read it again, especially the bit that he underlined. So I went with my mates into the park, our hair blowing in the breeze and our daisy chains around our necks. We sat down on the bench. I opened up the book and I said we might as well read it. There it was – all about love being patient, love being kind, love not being rude. I thought Dave was right – we hippies didn't have that kind of love; sure, nobody could have that kind of love. But I'll never forget Dave telling me that I could have a love like that if I had a relationship with Christ. But at that time, that was as far as I went with that deep theory.

I always think that, with addiction, you never believe it is actually happening to you. Addiction is like going down a hill. The first time you smoke a cigarette, or drink a pint of beer, or smoke a joint, you are standing at the top of that hill. You take a look at somebody who is a bit older than you and they are halfway down the hill and they have taken twice as much as you and you say to yourself that you'll never get as bad as that. But then there are those people who are farther on down the hill, near the bottom, who have taken twice as much again. They are looking back up, saying they'll never be as good as that again. That's another mistake. In general with addiction, we all tend to justify if we are addicted to something by looking at someone who takes a bit more of it than we do. That way we can feel good about ourselves.

To tell you the truth, if drink and drugs were not fun in the beginning, no one would ever have tried them. But they catch you, and they catch you so fast. The amazing thing about it is, you don't even realise when you are caught. If you had walked up to me in the first few years when I was drinking and taking drugs and asked me if I thought I had a problem, I would have told you, *of course I don't have a problem*, and to look at the man who lived around the corner, the alcoholic fella; now that was a guy with a *real* problem. You never believe it is going to happen to you, you think it is always going to happen to someone else, and I was no different.

My early drug education came in the shape of a young guy called Bug. Bug wasn't his real name, of course. He was short for his height; my mates and I were all afraid of standing on him, so we called him Bug. Teenagers can be cruel. One day, Bug asked me if I wanted to try some drug that he had. He told me it was cannabis. I asked him what it did. He said it would make me feel giddy and relaxed. On my lunch break from school, I ran home to get the money to pay for this bit of dope. There was nobody in our house and that was unfortunate. So there I was, I had no way to pay for this cannabis; then I had a bright idea. I slipped upstairs into my brother's bedroom and stole one of his LPs. I went back to Bug and swapped the record for another bit of dope. Bug then showed me how to roll my first joint, and I smoked that bit of dope. I thought it was the business; it made me feel just like he said it would, and I had no hangover from it, which was even better.

Later on, Bug introduced me to Black Bombers, which was another word for speed. He gave me two capsules and told me they would make me feel talkative and keep me awake all night. He gave them to me for nothing. As I was walking away he shouted at me to take only one of the capsules, and to get something to eat beforehand. I got home, opened up a can of cold rice, scooped it into me, took one of the capsules, waited five minutes . . . and nothing happened. I thought Bug had been winding me up and that probably nothing was going to happen. So I took the other one as well. Then I thought – that was a really dumb mistake. It was. Half an hour later it was like I had been plugged into an electric socket. I was high. I had thought that alcohol was good, cannabis had been good, but this, this was the *business*.

That night, still buzzing, I took my girlfriend to the cinema. The poor girl, we didn't see one bit of the movie. I came home, got into bed; everyone else was asleep and there I was sitting up in bed, wide awake. At dawn I was tiptoeing around the kitchen. My dad came down the stairs. I said good morning to him in a very deep voice. He wanted to know what I was doing up at that hour. I told him I was just getting ready for school, and that by the way I was really, really looking forward to school. I asked him if he wanted a cup of tea and a chat. Then, bright and early into school; I was prowling the corridors, looking around the place for anybody. I needed to express myself. I saw this teacher coming down the corridor. I disliked this teacher. In fact I hated him and he hated me. I started rambling on, saying good morning, that I thought we had a bit of a communication problem and that maybe we should sit down and talk about it. My day continued on erratically like that. That night, I was still buzzing. I kept thinking, when would this thing wear off? It eventually did, on the third day.

The drug itself was called Duraphet, because it was durable, and it was one of the most powerful speeds or amphetamines I could have taken. When it started to wear off those couple of days later, I felt sick and depressed, like I had been given a kicking. I promised myself I would never touch the stuff in future. Two weeks later, I started taking it again.

Now why did I do that? Why did I continually take drugs, even when I knew from my own experience that they were giving me a hard time? I think it was because I thought that I could always get it right the next time. I thought if I had just drunk a half bottle instead of a full bottle . . . or if I had just taken the beer and left the wine alone . . . or tried a different combination, then I might not have felt so bad. I told myself I would get it right the next time – get that combination that would give me the high without the low. But do you know what? I never found it. The further I looked, the more I got addicted.

I was always adamant that I was never going to become a junkie. Junkies put needles in their arms. I said I'd never do that. I had seen a guy on a television programme put a needle into his arm and it turned my stomach. I was frightened of needles and there was no danger of me being a junkie. I thought I was just going to smoke a bit of dope at the weekend and have a few beers. That's as far as it would go. And that's as far as it did go, for a while.

Chapter 5

We thought that, as hippies, we were the next big thing. We had an attractive philosophy – peace, love and understanding, man! For me, the drugs were just something that belonged on the edges of all this. The real reason I wanted to be a hippy was that I believed I was going to change society. So living this kind of life, it was a complete surprise and shock to our systems when the Troubles arrived.

Martin, Terry and I had Catholic friends and it never even entered our heads that there was a divide of any sort. We knew that the Catholics living among us went to a different church, but there was never a hint of trouble among us teenagers. There was nothing that would ever suggest what was about to happen to our community.

Though Lisburn was predominately a Protestant town, the relationships between people of all religions in that community were excellent. Maybe this was because we were at a distance from the main cities where there was more trouble. There were certainly big differences between us and places like Derry and Belfast, which saw the brunt of the violence and anger. Lisburn, by contrast, was a very well-mixed and healthy place, and it is even like that to this day. People in the Catholic and Protestant communities remained friends throughout the Troubles even though it was frowned upon.

Every Saturday night my mates and I went to a local club called The Jazzer, where we would buy our wee bits of dope. But as the weeks moved on, we began to see fewer of our usual friends in the usual haunts. Gradually we noticed that young people were leaving the North in their droves. We had seen the army tanks and jeeps coming down the streets and we knew deep down that we had to get out as well. It wasn't going to be a good place for a hippy. We'd seen patrols being set up and barbed wire being erected and we just thought: *This is not the place we want to be anymore*. It wasn't even a political decision; it was just an emotional one.

So, there we were, faced with the inevitable. For Martin, Terry and me it would be our first time to leave Ireland. Martin had just turned seventeen and I was lagging behind. Even though we dressed and thought we acted cool like hippies, at the same time we were still country boys at heart. It was 1970, and there was a lot of trouble brewing everywhere. Our intention was to go to England, to the Bath Festival of Blues and Progressive Music, a pop festival in a place called Shepton Mallet, near Glastonbury in Somerset. On that bill were going to be all the big names, such as Led Zeppelin and Pink Floyd. It was to be a three-day festival extravaganza for us hippies. In the end, we had to leave Martin at home as he tried but failed to persuade his dad to let him go with us. Martin had by this time left school and his parents had set him up in a job.

Terry and I left our parents with the notion that we would be going to the festival and maybe staying on for a while, but as far as they knew we didn't have any long-term plans. We just went with the intention of sussing it out, seeing what it was like and whether it would be possible for us to live there and stay away from Northern Ireland. That was the plan, if it could be called one. There were no big emotional farewells with our families; after all, they thought we were only going away for a few days.

We packed some clothes in a couple of cases, got the train to Belfast and then took the bus going out of Belfast to Aldergrove Airport. The bus had to make a detour because of a bomb scare. It travelled past the Royal Victoria Hospital on the Falls Road. I'll never forget what we saw there – on a stone wall, instead of the usual IRA victory slogans, someone had spray-painted the words "Sectarianism Kills Working Class People". Somebody of our ilk had obviously become a graffiti artist! As the bus continued towards the airport, we discussed this, and agreed with the graffiti artist. We knew it was people like us who were going to suffer from all of the violence. But thank God we were going to get out. It all made sense.

We flew in to Bristol Airport. On the way over, I was very nervous, because I had the tiniest little bit of dope on me, which I had bought the week before. Anybody who had given me more than a passing glance might have thought, from the way I was acting, that I was a major drug dealer! Once we landed, Terry and I had a heated debate, discussing who should carry the dope. I ended up carrying it, hiding it down my trousers, of all places. It was ridiculous – the amount was so tiny – but we turned it into a bigger deal than it actually was.

At the airport I noticed a couple of security people looking at us suspiciously. In those days, though, if you were Irish you were automatically thought of as suspicious, and luckily enough we didn't get stopped. When we got out of the airport we had to make our way to Shepton Mallet, where the festival was to start the next day. So, the good little country boys that we were, we thought we would check into a bed-and-breakfast. We headed to the nearest one carrying our overnight cases and booked in.

That night we went out to smoke our bit of dope and have a pint. It was our first culture shock; all we saw were Hells Angels and hippies everywhere. Nobody else was staying in bed-and-breakfasts; they were all sleeping in places like bus shelters or at the side of the roads. In many cases, they were not sleeping at all! Rather sheepishly, we went back to our bed-and-breakfast and crawled into our cosy beds, and the next morning we had a nice fry-up for breakfast. That was when it hit us; we felt so ridiculous, so conservative. Not like the hippies that we really were!

Then we heard the psychedelic music and suddenly we had this urge to get to the field where all the noise was coming from. We took the bus; the bed-and-breakfast landlady gave us directions. For the first half of the journey the bus travelled well but three or four miles from the festival grounds, the bus could hardly move. The road was covered by a sea of multicoloured waves with tens of thousands of young people, some decked in colourful garlands, all heading in the one direction. We got into the vibe quickly and, full of excitement, we jumped off the bus and mingled into the flowing hippy crowd.

We got washed along with the wave of enthusiasm. We could hear lots of excited shouts and calls, as the carnival atmosphere took over. The nearer we got to the field the greater the excitement was for us. As we went in, the first thing I heard was this buzz from the crowd, the humming pulse that told me everything was going to be cool. Some people approached us, calling out, "Hey, how you doing, man?!" At first we thought we must know half of them, until we realised this was the hippy culture being lived out, in the most extreme fashion. Everyone was everyone's best friend. It seems corny to say now, and looking back I know it was naivety on my part, but there was a real love in the air.

As we were getting our bearings I heard a voice coming out of the crowd: "Get your speed, get your dope, the cheapest you'll get, don't go any further." I looked up to where the voice was coming from; it seemed to be coming out of the sky. But then I looked harder and I saw this guy strapped by a rope onto the top of a telephone pole. There he was, lording it over all and he had these drugs, whatever you needed. Down at the bottom was a guy who took the money before the man on the pole passed down the purchases. We bought some speed and dope and it was quite cheap. So that was the beginning of the festival for us for the next three days. We were speeding out of our heads, and we were smoking dope.

Terry and I enthusiastically joined in with the other hippies. We were sitting in the middle of half a million others who were just like us. We spent the rest of the festival mooching around like zombies, out of our heads on drugs, watching and listening to the groups on stage. The odd time, we would have one of our deep and meaningful conversations. They usually went like this:

Me: "Wow, man!"

Terry: "Wow, yeah!"

That kind of conversation usually took three hours. It was intense. We were now part of that young generation of teenagers who were into their dope, living the hippy dream, loving the music and making friends. It was a stark contrast to what we had left back home. Was it any wonder that during those three days we made a decision not to return? Terry and I decided we were not going to leave our new all-embracing environment. It almost felt like a new world to us. So at this stage, my life was not at all terrible, and so what if the drugs were beginning to take over? The thing was, I just didn't realise how far they would go.

Chapter 6

Terry and I had been given a total immersion, a baptism, into the hippy culture. By the time we left the festival, we felt well and truly transformed into the real hippies that we always knew were lurking under our Northern Ireland exteriors.

Buoyant with this new-found life, we took a train into central London. We got out at Waterloo Station and found a space to sit on the platform, on top of our battered old suitcases, as we contemplated life and our next move. There we were, new-found hippies, sitting in our tie-dyed T-shirts with our long hippy hair and bell-bottomed jeans. We were surrounded by new noise and a sense of urgency, all these London commuters rushing past us. Instinctively we looked at each other. The contrast was shocking. Terry suddenly appeared very young and very confused. I asked him, "I suppose there is no chance that we can live there, you know, in that place where we've been?" Terry just lowered his head and shook it. "No, we can't," he said.

So we looked on, at the commuters, the pin-stripes running past us, and I thought, maybe this is it. Perhaps we could go and see our cleric friend Dave, who had moved to London. Maybe we could get a week staying with him, and then we'd just head back again, over the water, to what we knew. It didn't help that I was starting to feel a bit homesick, and Waterloo Station at rush hour was a scary and lonely place. People pushed past each other, and nobody treated anybody else like a human being.

We needed somewhere to stay and to see a friendly face. We decided to get the train up to where Dave was living in Norbiton in Kingston-upon-Thames. It was about eight miles from the centre of London itself, right on the edge of Surrey and the Greater London area. It was very posh indeed. I remembered at the time hearing that famous people, like the comedians Morecambe and Wise, lived in nearby Kingston Hill. It was also home to many politicians. Terry and I arrived like fish out of water.

We found Dave's address and I think he was glad to see us, if not a little concerned about any hidden motives we might have had. He put us up in his spare room. That night Dave was holding a Bible study group in his house. We got to know one or two of the young people there. Of course, we got to know the girls. Then one of the guys, Mark, who was a vicar's son, told us he could put us up in his parents' home for three weeks while they were away on holiday. It was music to our hippy ears. About a day after that, we moved into the quiet vicarage and had free rein of the place. We felt we had landed on our feet; we had been given an extra couple of weeks to enjoy our adventure in London.

Not wanting to waste the opportunity of living in close proximity to the centre of the city, Terry and I decided to take a trip in to Piccadilly in the hope of buying some dope. We were excited about it, even though we were totally new to the whole scene. I thought Piccadilly, or "the Dilly" as it was referred to by the cool hippies, was going to be the obvious place to buy drugs. It seemed so cosmopolitan and was full of hippies hanging around when we came up from the tube station.

A guy came over to us and asked, "Do you want to score?"

I said, "Yeah."

"You've got to follow me quickly because the drug squad are everywhere," he said.

It seemed very dramatic and covert, but it was all part of a plot, which we didn't realise at the time. So we followed this guy into the tube station and he said, "Quickly! Quickly! How much do you want?"

And we said, "Eh . . . ten pounds' worth."

We gave him the money and he shoved a brown bag into our hands and rushed off. We were looking at it, laughing: "Wow, this is the place! Good value – there seems to be a lot here!" We opened the bag and looked in at some sort of green powder. I'd never seen dope like that before. So we went back to the vicarage and put it into a joint and started to smoke it, and suddenly all these little sparks started flying out of it. I think it was curry powder.

But that didn't put us off! The following week we thought we'd try again, so we went back down to the Dilly. This time we saw a guy standing there with two or three people around him, mostly tourists who were buying dope – and we could see that the dope he was handing out looked like the real deal. So we confidently walked over to him and asked if we could score some. He just looked at us and asked, "Are you kids from Belfast?" We said, "Yeah", to look cool and to save hassle. He said, "Take a tip, kids. Go back to wherever you're staying and don't try to score in Piccadilly. Piccadilly's for the tourists." So, nodding like we understood and giving him a wink, we sauntered on back to the tube station. We took it that we had arrived!

Our search for drugs continued. Things improved when we heard about a pub called The Three Fishes in Kingston-upon-Thames. It was a huge two-storey establishment. This became our hippy Mecca. There were probably about a thousand young people there every weekend. It was also full every night of the week. The place did attract a lot of "plastic hippies" – that was the name we gave to the type of hippy who was only a weekend hippy, the kind of guy who put his suit back on for work on the Monday morning. The mainstay in The Three Fishes would have been the real hippies, all out living in squats. Squats had become a great idea, where people would take over property and live in it rent-free. Squats, to our minds, stuck close to the hippy ideal of sharing the wealth. Terry and I would become regulars at The Three Fishes and managed to score our dope there.

But Dave was keeping a close eye on us. I am not sure if he realised how far our foray into the London drug scene had gone. One morning he stormed into our room with his black clerical robes flying behind him. He looked like he meant business. He was mad with us. He told us to get up and start looking for jobs if we were to stay. All Terry and I could do was lift our heads, say "Yeah man", and drop them back down on the pillows. For the moment, we were not moving. We felt we were not harming anyone; we were just being hippies and experiencing life.

We made all sorts of false promises to our parents at home regarding how we were living in this big posh vicarage, where of course we made ourselves well and truly at home. This gave us time to persuade Martin to come and join us. We were constantly on the phone to him, annoying him. Usually it was me saying, "Man, you don't know what you're missing. This is what happened at the festival, now we've found a pub called The Three Fishes. We are not coming back so you've gotta come."

We'd barrage him every night. Sometimes we phoned him up stoned, just to make him jealous. We told him we were living the hippy dream, that we had found girls already, from the Bible study group, and they were interested in us because we were not English. We told Martin there was plenty more where that came from, so why not come on over? I guess we put enough pressure on because Martin and his dad eventually had a big bust-up over him leaving. But Martin walked out of his house and travelled over to London. We met him at Heathrow. The Three Musketeers were finally reunited.

One day Dave was having a Bible study group meeting. We were sitting in his kitchen and he came in and asked us if we wanted to join in. We kept silent. I think it broke his heart to see that we were so into our hippy lifestyle.

We did, after all, think that it was the answer to everything and that God played no part in it. By this stage we were fully fledged hippies, all the beads and bells and all that paraphernalia. But finally one night, we caved in. We went into Dave's front room and joined the handful of young people who were very much into their religion and God.

At the beginning of the meeting everyone was friendly and the talk was general, about life, death and so on. But then the discussion broadened out from Bible study, and went through to the whole idea of Christianity and belief systems. I looked at Terry and he started talking, holding centre stage. He had really come out of his shell since he arrived in London and he was hammering the hippy message through to these Bible study kids. He asked, "Why are you wasting time with this? Why don't you turn on, tune in, drop out, and become part of the real revolution?"

I was sitting right beside him, but I began to hold back with my opinions, even though I was wholeheartedly supporting him. The irony of it was, a year later Terry decided to give up the hippy way of life and follow Christ and believe in Him. So, of the three of us, the one who was most against Christianity was the one who would fall first for the Lord.

Funnily enough, before that, Terry told us there was no way he was going back to Northern Ireland. It had been the same for Martin. I said, "Well if we are sure, let's give it a go."

So we found out about available bedsits from one of the girls in the Bible study group.

Chapter 7

A short time later, we moved into 75 Gloucester Road, Kingston-upon-Thames. Our landlady, Mrs Gari, was Pakistani and she had every part of the house rented out. She lived in one room with her husband and children. There were two levels to the house. We got the biggest room, but there were only two beds in it. We told her we didn't want to be separated and convinced her to put another bed into the room.

Martin, Terry and I were now enjoying life. It was real freedom for us. Of course, we were only living in a one-room bed-sit, but it was up to us to decide when we went to bed, if we went to bed. We could ask people to visit, or not. The choices were endless! Because we were so young and caught up in the whole hippy thing, the kids from the church whom we had met had never seen anything like us before. For a while we probably came across a bit like pop stars to them. We had long hair, talked with a different accent and were really chilled out. They started visiting us in the bed-sit and, of course, we encouraged them to come along.

And that's where most of our funding came from. In the first couple of months we had an entourage of about twenty of these kids visiting us, and I would say to them, "You are welcome to come here, but we have no money. We need to make this week's rent, can you help support us?" Those young people paid our rent for weeks and weeks. We initially didn't even have the brains to sign on, as at this point we were also still living off the couple of pounds that my mum kept sending over from home. We eventually got onto social security and then I went out into the big bad world of grown up work. I got a job as an accounts clerk for a local building firm, J.M.W. Mayer. Terry went to work in a factory and Martin went onto the building sites. In the beginning, I was thinking, *This is great, now we'll have a nice sensible life.*

Terry became friendly with a group of Christian artists who lived in the bed-sit on the ground floor. Being a painter himself, he began spending more time in their company and he rarely came out socialising with us. This was the beginning of the split in our relationship with him.

One night Martin and I went down to The Three Fishes. We were having a drink and smoking a bit of blow, when in walked a guy called Steve Cooper. Steve was of German descent and his parents worked as a cook and a waitress in one of the top hotels in Richmond. He even lived above the hotel. Steve started to talk to us and he asked us if we had ever tried LSD. He took out a tiny little tablet called Blue Cheer, broke it and gave us half each. He said not to worry about paying him and that he would stay with us throughout the trip.

As we left the pub and were walking with Steve, the LSD really started to work. It was a new feeling for me, and it was almost indescribable. The first thing I noticed was that my body started to feel very tingly. There was warmth in me as if somebody had just switched on the central heating. I thought this was as high as it was going to get, and it was great. Steve told us he would take us to some guy he knew who lived nearby.

On the way there the drugs squad stopped us. As the cops were asking me my address I could feel the LSD coming up for real. I just managed to get my address out, and they let us go. As we walked off down the road, by now my trip was fully up. When we got to this house, which was more like a penthouse, I was so high that I thought the front door was waving at me. We went inside and met the guy who owned the house, whose name was Dom. He was a hippy, but he obviously specialised in looking after people who were on their first trip. Steve said, "These are two first timers." Dom just said, "Come on, sit down." He was very kind and guided us through it. I definitely needed the guidance!

Martin sat down, put on a pair of headphones, listened to some music and went away to The Moody Blues. But I was sitting in the other corner and I was so frightened, trying not to let it show. I didn't like the feeling that something had taken control of me. Some of the hallucinations were awful. I was looking at Jimi Hendrix on a poster, and I started to see his head fall off, and roll across the carpet towards me. Steve kept saying into my ear, "Man, it's like turning on a water tap full blast and then putting a cork in it. You are fighting it. You need to let it go; otherwise you will have a really bad time." Dom called me over. He picked up a sheet of paper and a pen and said, "Just watch this." He started drawing lines on the paper. Gradually he drew a blossoming tree, and the more leaves that grew on that tree, the happier I became. By the time it was in full blossom, he was finished, my trip was out, and I was stone cold sober.

When I looked around I saw that the house was full of people; some were on speed, some on dope, but the majority were on LSD. Dom had made sure that every eventuality was covered. He even had old gaming machines, like old slot machines, fixed onto some of the walls, so people could play a couple of games while they were tripping. Because it was the weekend and we had no work until Monday, we took another trip and spent most of the next day there, still tripping.

By this stage Martin was singing the praises of LSD but I wasn't so sure about it. I was praying to the Lord for the first time in ages to get me through it. And sure enough, after a day, it finally finished. In those days it was pure LSD, not adulterated in any way, and it was very powerful stuff. Of course I never kept my promise; I did try it later on. I took it on maybe twenty other occasions, but I would take half of whatever Martin was having. He could handle it, I couldn't. I was more into speed.

Chapter 8

When I was seventeen years old, my parents first found out that I was on drugs for real. The whole LSD experience was so overwhelming for me that, naively, I wrote a letter home to my brother Raymond, in which I went into great detail about the positive and negative effects. I wrote because I needed to tell somebody about the trips. Unfortunately, mum intercepted the letter at home. So that's how my mother first found out that her youngest son was taking drugs.

Even though I was in London, I still felt a strong bond with my family back home. I loved them enough not to want to hurt them. I remember sitting in the accounts office at J.M.W. when a phone call came through for me. It was dad. He was ringing from Stormont, where he had secured a job as a civil servant. In the early fifties he had a job in the law courts and then he had worked his way up in Stormont. He had been a civil servant who looked after the needs of the Prime Minister's office.

Dad was on the other end of the phone, saying, "Jackie, I just want you to pack up your things and get on the next plane home, and let your mother see you, right now." I wasn't sure what to do. I told Mr Mayer that I had to go home straight away, that there was a family crisis. I wasn't far wrong. He held the job open for me, so I could go home. I was so shocked by my father's phone call and the bond was so great between us that I did pack my bags and get on the first plane home. I wasn't going to let my mother be heartbroken. My parents still had that hold on me, because I loved them.

Once I got home to Lisburn, I sat around the house for nine weeks. The atmosphere wasn't too good. I spent many of those weeks telling my parents, swearing blind, that if they let me go back to London, I would work harder and never touch any drugs again. Because I was so adamant, they let me go. In reality, I could have gone at any time; after all, I had a job and I was over sixteen. But I had to reassure them, so I told them what I thought they wanted to hear. From their point of view, they needed to think that this was a once-off, that it was never going to happen again. In any case, they probably reasoned, I was keeping a job down. What parent would think for a moment that their child would be able to work and still take trips on LSD? So, with both sides somewhat reluctant, I managed to convince them. Unspoken in all of this, part of me was really saying to them: *There's nothing either of you can do, but I just don't want to break up with you.*

For those nine weeks when I was home I thought

about getting drugs but it was difficult to go anywhere without someone going with me. It would have been a fruitless search anyway because by this time Northern Ireland was under siege. In the earlier days, when I had started taking drugs at home, it had become more and more difficult to get them. They were not plentiful. So I was weaning myself off the drugs during the stay at home. When I decided to go back to London, I didn't have any great heartbreak about it. To my mind, I was determined not to take any more LSD.

In reality, though, I wanted to hold onto the lifestyle: going to The Three Fishes, acting the hippy, having the craic. And I thought, *I haven't really hurt my parents*; in my mind, they had gotten over it, that it was just a once-off, a blip. But I was fooling myself. I was convinced that what I was selfishly doing was right and that it didn't hurt anybody else. Wrong: *I* was the one who wanted to be part of that scene. I wanted to be the guy who smoked dope and took pills. I wanted to believe that I would never be hooked. At the end of the day, I thought, *I'm in control*.

Chapter 9

Gloucester Road became a Mecca for young people who knew the two Irish guys who could get drugs for them. We never considered ourselves to be drug dealers; we only ever thought of it as a friendship thing. We might make a couple of pounds from it to pay the rent. In fact, we could have made a huge amount of money if we had thought about it properly. But the word *profit* was not in our dictionary. We stuck to the hippy philosophy: everybody needed drugs to enjoy life. Those without them were little misfortunates; we needed to help these poor children find a better way of life. It was almost like a mission: we would give people drugs for free. But this was ignorance; I can see now that this was another delusion. We didn't realise at the time what we were doing, and we certainly didn't see the consequences ahead, not only for us, but for those we gave drugs to.

My need for drugs moved up a gear; it changed from

becoming a weekend thing to an everyday thing. I had an overpowering urge to get more and more drugs. I became fanatical about them. They were my life.

Of course, at no time did I ever think that I was addicted. That never entered my head. I made a definite conscious decision to stop just mucking around casually with drugs and giving them out to friends. The drugs would no longer be only a social aside to my life. I wanted to make them the centrepiece. I longed for that every day.

I wasn't addicted; I was just in love with drugs. And this was good love – or so I thought. I believed my life was on the up and that the drugs would elevate me further into an even more fantastic life, a life I could only have dreamed of. I was looking for that higher high. I wanted it all. I honestly thought I was *the* man on the drugs scene – that everyone was just in awe of me and couldn't get enough of me. Maybe somewhere at the back of my mind I might have thought, *these people, these hangers-on, are only really with me for the drugs.* But it didn't matter. I didn't understand that, as the numbers of my so-called friends grew and grew, the further down I was sinking into the depths of my addiction. I was completely unaware that I was sentencing myself to a life of total reliance on these drugs.

To keep feeding my growing desire in my new love relationship, I decided to make some contacts to see if we could get some more drugs to sell. I arranged to meet Martin one Saturday at Kingston Railway Station. He had been visiting his girlfriend, Caroline. We were going to meet a guy called Paul Arrowsmith, who was a local dealer and was very much "in the know". He was very proactive in the drugs scene and was one of the top dealers in the area. I was hoping to buy some speed and some cannabis off him. I was going to sell most of it and of course keep some for "recreational purposes". It was our first meeting and it was very important. And like any business meeting – especially the first time – you want to make a good impression.

So when Martin bounced off the train with a huge smiley face on him and glazy eyes, I was a bit worried. I asked him, "What are you on?" And he said, "I'm trippin' on LSD." I groaned, "Oh, great!" We went around to Arrowsmith anyway. He had a flat above a fish-and-chip shop that he owned and that his girlfriend ran. He sold the drugs from the flat. Paul had long ringleted hair and a rugged face. He was originally from Jersey and his father was a doctor. Paul was speed-mad; he loved amphetamine sulphate and he loved to talk. I had warned Martin, "Look, you can just come around to this chip shop with me. I'll go and meet this guy by myself; you stay downstairs, and don't give any trouble." Martin smiled and assured me everything would be fine. We went in. I went under the counter, up the stairs to meet Arrowsmith to discuss how much money he wanted for the drugs and how much we were prepared to pay. But just five minutes into my chat with him, I heard this girl screaming in the shop. I came downstairs in double-quick time with Arrowsmith running ahead of me. We found this poor employee standing behind the counter, a terrified look on her face. Martin had seen a chicken roasting in the glass oven. He had got so caught up in it that he had leapt the counter, took the chicken out and was standing in the middle of the shop eating the whole thing, right in front of her.

Arrowsmith was not amused. I was quick to apologise; after all, this was my partner in crime. Arrowsmith was hesitant. He said, "Well it's not on man, you know." I said, "I promise you, I will take him home with the chicken. We'll pay for it, and I'll see you again." Arrowsmith was cool with this. So I took Martin up towards Gloucester Road. He was carrying a plastic bag and the hot chicken inside was slowly melting it away. I berated him about what an exhibition he had made out of us. How could we be treated as serious dealers if he was going to do silly things like that? Martin was still smiling, saying, "Chill out man, don't worry about it."

Just then, as we approached Gloucester Road, I saw Kev, another one of our friends, walking across the main road with a huge framed painting under his arm. Terry had painted it; he had become quite the artist. But Kev wouldn't leave it in his flat because the woman in the painting looked like his girlfriend and he was missing her. Kev was high and had got a fixation about it. He took it into the local newsagent with him to buy some cigarettes. People were spilling out of the front of Gloucester Road, laughing at the spectacle. The cops were driving up and down the street. The police station was very close to us on Gloucester Road. How we never got busted was a mystery to me.

I thought: it's time to move. The next day, I said to Martin, "We gotta get out of here, it's getting too hot, too obvious." So we started to look for a flat.

Mrs Gari had been very tolerant. What she didn't know was that we kept the drugs out in the open in a corner of the bed-sit. She might have had her suspicions with the number of people traipsing in and out of her house at all times of the day to get to our room. Eventually things started to get out of hand, with late night, early morning parties. Mrs Gari warned us to cut down on the social life.

I was still working in J.M.W. It was eight months on and I was doing really well in the firm, so much so that Mr Mayer himself wrote out a cheque for a month's rent in advance when we started looking for a new flat. Things were going well; we had a whole new horizon ahead of us. But then Martin got the sack from the building site and I was pretty fed up with this. In a way I thought I had been holding us all together. Martin going on the dole was the last straw, the excuse I needed not to go to work. In any case when the drugs were around, I had two choices: go to work, or party. The two couldn't mix. Besides, there was really no contest – the drugs won all the time.

When I was partying I would take speed and stay up until dawn, sometimes even staying up two or three days in a row. I had done the best out of the three of us at the beginning because I had a clerical job and I was able to arrive into work, slide in behind the desk, do a bit of pen pushing and come home. But the other two had more physical jobs. However, Martin getting the sack came at the right time. We were making connections with pushers who were selling larger amounts of drugs. We were getting them cheaper, and we were eventually making more money. On a good week we could make up to £1,000.

We left our jobs and started to pay our rent and our living expenses out of the profits from the drugs. Terry decided to stay with Mrs Gari and moved into a flat downstairs. So Martin and I had a choice to make, and we wanted a bigger place than the bed-sit. We needed to get a flat, somewhere smart to operate from. Mrs Gari was in full agreement when we told her we had to move. We came to an agreement with her that as soon as we found a place, we would move out, and miraculously we left on good terms.

We found a flat that suited on Manor Gate Road, just a few streets away. It was far superior to the bed-sit – it was ideal. Not only did it have a front entrance, it also had a back entrance with French windows that led out onto an alleyway. So there was a quick escape route from any curious police should we ever need it. Of course, that never entered our minds, because we thought: *We'll never be busted; we'll never be arrested.*

Chapter 10

We became street dealers. The dealing had become quite a major part of our lives. It paid for the rent. I took jobs sporadically, but as the drugs worked, everything took second place. I didn't see the drugs as others did; I thought they were the greatest thing since sliced bread. I thought no one could enjoy life if they weren't high. I still had a missionary zeal, almost a sense of "joy" about cannabis, speed and LSD – and I had to convert the willing listeners to it. In truth, I was a kid and I was naive.

We now more or less had the run of The Three Fishes. We had become secondary dealers there, where we had a very large clientele. We also extended our drugs empire to include another supplier who was able to source drugs from a local chemist. In those days, there were restrictions on the sale of amphetamines, or on DDA drugs – in other words, those listed under the Dangerous Drugs Act. But amphetamines were still being handed out by some doctors. So it wasn't unusual if our supplier got an extra order for 300 here or there. When they were delivered to the shops, our supplier would just put the extra bottles into a bag, and come home with them to our flat. That's how we got our quality speed – and came to the attention of a guy nicknamed Nash, who supplied most of Surrey with cannabis, amphetamines and LSD.

Nash was the man that everybody went to, whether they knew it or not. He was in his thirties and looked like a Viking with long blonde straw-like hair, a similar beard, and piercing blue eyes. He had obviously done a lot of physical work in his earlier days; he was well built and well able to look after himself. He worked alongside this little woman, nicknamed Mum. She looked like a nice old lady; she wore a headscarf and carried her shopping bags everywhere.

Contrary to what we had heard, Nash did not come across as menacing – at least initially. The day we met him, we were sitting in The Three Fishes, selling cannabis and LSD and having a pint. This guy came over, sat down and introduced himself.

"I'm Nash, and I hear that you guys can get some quality speed?"

We thought he was a punter. I took to him straight away. I said, "Ah yeah, what would you like?"

"What can you get me?"

"I can get you anything."

This impressed him, especially when I put my hand in my pocket and brought out some dexamphetamine – Treble Decks, they were called; large capsules of amphetamines that would keep you going for a couple of days. So I gave him some. He paid me a couple of pounds.

The next night he was back again, looking for more. He invited us to his house. Before we went there, people in the pub were saying: "Do you know who that was? He's the guy, he's the man." So we obviously saw this as a great opportunity. We were going up a level. We had already bought plenty of dexamphetamine and we had our new chemist supplies as well. We had purchased our cannabis from a guy called Scottish Johnny. It turned out he had sourced his supplies from some guy who was big, but we never realised until that night that it was actually Nash. So then we cut out our middleman, and we were able to go straight to the source.

Despite all the wheeling and dealing, I still wanted to keep the social side alive, the hippy dream, and for me it really was not all about profit. When I was involved in dealing, I had so many people who wanted to be in my company, to use my drugs and pay me money for them. I didn't need to look for first-timers. I never forced anyone to take drugs.

With one exception. We had a friend called Michael. He smoked cannabis when we met him, but he had never taken speed. Michael was probably one of the quietest guys I had ever met. Nobody could get a word out of him. So I thought that the most incredible thing I could do for Michael would be to give him some speed. I finally talked him into trying some. He took his tabs, sat the same as before . . . didn't speak . . . didn't utter a word. I asked him, "Don't you feel it?"

"Yeah."

"Is there anything you want to say?"

"Nope."

And that's the way it went for two nights. Until the third night, I gave him some more, and something happened and we couldn't shut him up! But that was the only time that I ever deliberately sat someone down and gave them drugs. I introduced people to other drugs, drugs that they were already looking for.

Chapter 11

I was approaching my eighteenth birthday and was about to become a registered drug user on the National Health. I had heard from some people on the "scene" about a doctor who was willing to prescribe large amounts of drugs. This doctor was on his own naive crusade to wean "desperadoes" off drugs. He had a surgery nearby and this was too good an opportunity for me to miss.

But I thought that this doctor might take one look at me, and decide I might not have been far enough down that road for saving. So to cover all bases I phoned up my cleric friend Dave Burnel and spun him a yarn about how I was truly sick of drugs and wanted more than anything else in the world to come off them. Dave was really supportive and said he would go to this doctor with me the next day.

I thought this was great; I was going to get free drugs and have Dave as a cast-iron referee. In we went the next day. I looked around the waiting room. All heads turned to us. It was like the front lounge of The Three Fishes. I recognised half the faces. "Hey, man!" someone said, making the peace sign with his fingers. "Yeah, hey!" I called back, suddenly feeling a bit uncomfortable about going to the doctor with a man of the cloth.

When the time came, we went into the doctor's surgery and I began to lament about how the drugs were ruining my life, that I wanted to get back on to the straight and narrow. Dave was nodding all the time, agreeing. He told the doctor I was sincere. I didn't care that I was lying. My conscience was clear because I believed I wasn't addicted. I thought I could call a halt to it at any stage. I did not believe I was harming Dave. I was not duping my friend.

So I poured my heart out to this doctor:

"I can't hack it, man. I need something to get me off these things."

"Well, I can only prescribe some new drugs which may help."

"Great, doctor. I'll take anything, as long as it helps me."

I returned to that doctor a few more times without Dave and eventually he decided to register me with the NHS as drug-dependent. That meant any doctor was now under an obligation to treat me. If a doctor decided he was unwilling to prescribe, I was merely passed onto someone else who would. My registration was a major stepping stone for me into everyday drug use, and it reinforced my desire for drugs.

Martin and I had taken over from two of the top dealers out of The Three Fishes. They had decided to give it up; they had been doing it for three years before we had arrived, but their business had fallen apart because we were doing so well. There were no hard feelings; I think they just had had enough of it. Now we started to deal for the whole of the pub and the wider customer base. The drugs had firmly become my daily fix; they were not recreational anymore. They were the main source of my income and my life support.

These were the good days, the days when I was Jack the Lad, Number One. We would arrive in the pub, and the girls would take my arm as I came through the door. They would say, "How are you, man? Great to see you!" I felt like a pop star. By now I had a hundred friends who would have sat with me, who would have died to be in my company. I never thought for a moment that it was anything to do with the fact that they wanted my drugs. I thought, really foolishly, that they were just pleased to be with me, that they wanted to be in my company because I was so popular. I would look around the pub, full of punters, everyone high and in great form – drink flowing, girls hanging onto my every word, and I would think: *This is my kingdom, my world.* But sometimes, in the middle of it all, other thoughts would come back to me: *Is this it? Is that all there is?*

We didn't want to repeat the mistakes we had made when we were living in Gloucester Road, so we kept the majority of visitors to our flat to a small nucleus of about fifteen people – our closest friends. The remainder were our social friends who liked to spend time in our company. We figured this was because we were an exciting novelty – we weren't English, we were Irish. We had come to their country, their town, and we were dealers and able to provide them with what they wanted.

Our parties in the new flat were very laid-back affairs. There would usually be fifteen young people in the flat along with Martin and myself. The room would have the usual trappings of incense sticks burning off mellow perfumes. We also had our red lightbulbs, hippy music playing on the stereo and guests sitting around cross-legged, others lying over beds, some getting ready to crash, some leaving and some returning to the party. But in the middle of all of this, if you had looked carefully, you would have seen books on Buddhism, philosophy and faith, even a Bible. I certainly was still searching for something, though at the time I wasn't aware of it. I had a great interest in the idea of religion, in the big question: What is God? I never really got to a place during the drug-taking where I completely shook off the belief that there had to be something more to my life.

God never really got a say in anything. I would have conversations and philosophical debates about Him, but that was all. At one of our drug-fuelled parties I even drew a diagram for the attending audience of young people. I drew a spoked wheel, with lines coming out of it. "You have Buddhism here, the Muslim religion here and the Christian religion here, and it's all attached to the one God," I said, staring down at a crowd of stoned hippies. I suppose it was new age philosophy before it was ever called that. But this God of mine was great. He didn't ask me to do anything. It was very convenient. I could draw a diagram about Him, I could talk about Him, but He wouldn't interfere with my drug-taking. Now this was the kind of God I liked!

As the drugs continued to work they managed to keep the feelings of emptiness and isolation away, for a while. It helped that I now had a steady girlfriend, Anna. She was sweet sixteen, with long blonde hair, and she was still at school. I would meet her at the school gates most days. I had first spotted her in Gloucester Road, when she came in one night to the Christian artists' group who lived at the bottom of the house, the group Terry ended up with. I asked about her through different people. It was all very childishly innocent. I let the girlfriend of one of my mates know that I was interested in her and this contact came back and told me that she was interested in me too. So we met, went out and started to "go steady". We were to last the distance for almost two years.

Anna was not really into drugs. She experimented very lightly with cannabis. But of course, because it was part of my life, she started to experiment with more cannabis and speed. She didn't get caught up in the drugs, though; she was caught up in me, and I was caught up in her and the drugs. So, Anna was with me, Martin was with Caroline and we had this nucleus of friends, Bill, Kev, John, Ken, Liza and Michael. We were all set.

Even though we had become known to Nash, Martin and I had also become known to the police. While we were visiting his flat, buying all the gear at a cheaper rate, gaining more customers, the police began to wake up to "the two Irish guys".

One night we came back from The Three Fishes to find the Drugs Squad waiting in our flat for us. We went in and they were standing in the middle of the living room with a police dog. They had Anna, Caroline and Kev all imprisoned there until we had arrived. Now the cops had made a couple of major mistakes that night. First of all they should have arrested Martin and me as soon as we had arrived at the pub, because we had a lot more drugs on us at that point. But it had been a good night and we had sold most of what we had brought with us. So when we came back we only had about three or four ten-pound deals of cannabis left, a couple of packets of dex and a few tabs of LSD, all for our personal use. The second mistake was that the dog the squad had with them was just a little Labrador puppy, and I think they were trying to train it. At one stage it wouldn't go under Martin's bed to find anything, so they kicked it. The poor little thing came out with a little bit of silver paper in its mouth, and they patted it on the head, pleased with this.

What amazed me most was that the whole time they were chatting to us, taking details down and letting us know our rights, they were stepping over kettles, cups, plates, knives and they never once said, "Where is your kitchen?" If they had, they would have walked across the little corridor, opened the food cupboard and there would have been somewhere in the region of 5,000 dexamphetamine tablets, a whole bunch of hundreds of LSD and about three or four ounces of cannabis. They missed the bigger picture.

Martin and I were arrested. When Kev saw what was happening, he did the most amazing thing. Kev said, "What about me?" And the cops said, "What do you mean, what about you?" Kev said, "Well, a third of the stuff that you've got off the guys is mine. Aren't you going to arrest me?" So they obliged and arrested him. To us, it was a sign of friendship. People did crazy things like that in those hippy days.

So Kev stood with Martin and myself in Kingston Magistrates Court on 15 March 1972, and got sentenced for something that he didn't even need to be there for. But that was the kind of friend we had. I was fined £10 for possessing cannabis resin, another £10 for possessing LSD and I was given the Probation Order for two years for possessing amphetamines. I was sent on remand for a month. Before it had come to sentencing, we were still so proud of the fact that we had got one over on the police, we never for a moment thought about stopping dealing.

Chapter 12

The first time I saw the inside of a prison was at the age of nineteen – all because we had been busted for having drugs, rather than for dealing them. Martin and I were remanded in custody, but because we were juveniles we were sent to Ashfield Remand Centre in Kent, a very formidable old red-brick building, almost Victorian in style. It might as well have been in the middle of nowhere.

It was a very tough regime. The ethos was, *Get them in young and teach them a hard lesson.* When we arrived at the reception we were stripped naked by the warders; we weren't allowed to wear our own clothes. We stood in line with the other young men, and to keep what modesty we had, we ended up standing like a row of footballers making up a defensive wall. We were then painted with a white mixture, which was to protect us from a dose of the scabies that was rife in there at the time. We were given rough prison clothes to wear and frogmarched down to the cells. We were also given our blankets and sheets and we made our own beds. Martin and I were separated immediately, put into two different cells.

The first thing I noticed when I got into my cell was the bunk bed on the left and a single bed on the right. Most cellmates usually try to get the single or the top bunk for more privacy. I ended up with the single, and I shared the cell with an English guy called Gary, whose dad seemed to have connections with the prison authorities. As we settled down to sleep that night, the spy hole, or the Judas Hole as it is called, was opened and we could feel a warder looking through. Then he opened the cell door just wide enough to throw in some tobacco. My cellmate told me his father had paid for it on the outside.

I was in the dark from half past seven in the evening when they put the lights out. It was my first time in a cell, and when the door slammed for the night, there was no sound quite like it – it had a sound and feeling all of its own. It was incarceration in every sense. Not only was I locked in there, but I knew that if anything happened to me in the cell, I'd have little or no chance. There was a bell on the wall but nobody ever answered it; all the prisoners knew this. If you needed assistance, if you were ill, for instance, you would have to shout. I felt helpless, as if I was a rabbit caught in the headlights. I was in shock and it was like a bad dream.

In the morning I was up at six o'clock. In the light of day, the cell was grey and miserable. There was a window high up with bars on it. I took the trouble to pull myself up to see the view outside, and all I could see was the exercise yard. There were no views of the country or the hills beyond the remand centre. There was no walking along in the park hand-in-hand with Anna; no dad to say everything would be alright; and at night there would be no mum to wish me goodnight. There was nothing, except the realistic, depressing thought that I might actually be spending a long time here.

Everything was routine – military fashion was the best way to describe it. Most of the warders wore their peaked caps right down over their noses. They were like military police rather than warders. You didn't walk anywhere; you were marched everywhere. On my first morning, I was marched down for breakfast. Then I was brought before the Prison Governor. Here I met up with Martin again. The Governor asked our names and if we knew why we were there. Then we were handed over to this stocky guy with a shaven head and he went through our offences. He told us why we had been remanded and how long we were to stay – which was as long as a piece of string; it depended on whether we got bail. It was very frightening for me because I had never seen anything like this before, and everything was being taken out of my hands. The warder looked dismissively at us, with our long hair, standing in prison uniforms. He glanced at the file, at the charge of possession, and he said, "So you are in for drugs. Why on earth are you not back in Northern Ireland fighting for your country?" At this point Martin and I burst out laughing, which didn't go down too well with him. He said, "Shut up! What are you laughing for?" Being a bit lippy and always wanting to volunteer an answer, I was the first to say, "Why would we want to go back there and fight for peace when we can end up here?" He said, "If you were real men, that is what you would be doing." Martin then piped up, "I guess we are not real men then." It was all very surreal; I stood beside my best mate in those dreadful prison clothes, in the worst place I ever wanted to be and wondered: *How did a hippy like me get here?*

We were promptly marched back to our own cells.

Later that day I was given a crash course in how to make my bed – military fashion. Every corner was tucked in so I could bounce a penny off it.

Then I noticed the three small plastic potties at the end of the cell, handy for emergencies. During the day we were allowed to go to the canteen to get our food and bring it back into the cell. In that brief moment, you had about fifteen minutes to run to the main toilet and use it. You had to be back in your cell before the warders would shout, "Lock up!" So that meant if you were halfway through something, you had to go – you had to run. If you didn't do that, you had what were called "brown parcels" to take back to the cell with you!

The next morning, you had to be careful where you stood in the exercise yard as there were brown parcels all over the ground. Somebody would then be given the job of cleaning them up. It sounds funny, but it wasn't. It was all to do with humiliation. But I gained strength from other prisoners who had been in before. They kept us right.

There were so many minute things, all aimed at trying to break your spirit. A simple thing like cutting my toenails turned into a drama. I hadn't got around to cutting them before I was sent on remand, because I was stoned. I had to apply through one warder, then to the Head Warder in order to get something to cut them with – and I was put on a waiting list. I was actually notified when I was allowed to cut my toenails! One day I was given a big pair of clippers, almost like hedge-cutters – they didn't give out scissors for obvious reasons. So that was an experience!

There was real tension in the air, all the time, at Ashfield. I kept my head down, did my work, ate my meals and learned how to survive, especially on the cigarette rations. I would get a quarter of an ounce of tobacco, which would have to last a week. This was my wages for chopping pieces of wood into logs. The first week I worked, I had no tobacco. I had to roll my cigarettes out of what they called the sweepings. Every morning the inmates had to sweep out their cell. So I would run along the corridor and see if anybody had swept out a tiny little roll of butt and then gather them up and smoke them. This was the first week in a long time that I was without drugs of any sort, apart from these bits of cigarettes. I couldn't let this get to me because remand was hard enough to do and I needed to keep my head fixed. So I survived the first week on sweepings and from getting the odd smokes from my cellmate.

The second week I got my first week's wages. I thought I would be able to get half an ounce of tobacco, cigarette papers and matches. Wrong; I got a quarter ounce and only enough money to buy either cigarette papers or matches – not both. It was part of the breaking-your-spirit regime. My solution was to buy the matches one week and cigarette papers the next. I'd get the loan of a razor blade from some other prisoner. It was a hard-backed razor blade used for cutting up deals, but this time I was cutting up matches. I sliced each match in four – just to have enough for the next week. I had to find ways to distract my desire for my drugs.

There was a mobile library service in the prison, which really consisted of someone going around offering books to us inmates. I spent time in my cell reading; unlike some of the other prisoners who couldn't read, I was fortunate. I remember I got a book about this little idyllic village in England somewhere, where a young man came to live and I remember thinking that I would love to be that man, especially now that I was in a cell. In the book, he would go to the pub in the evenings, where the genial host would give him a pint, but it would never be more than he could handle and his life seemed just so together. In contrast, Martin had got his hands on J.R.R. Tolkien's *The Lord of the Rings*, and he spent his time, a full month, reading it. Typical Martin – he was just fascinated with surreal worlds. So that is how we did our time.

Before Ashfield, I would usually get a weekly letter from mum and would send some little note back to her. Of course, she was not aware of my situation. My main anxiety in the first couple of days at Ashfield was the approaching Mother's Day. My all-consuming concern was that my parents didn't find out I was in prison. But I was going to have to send mum a card and there was no way I could do it from prison. Luckily Caroline and Anna came to visit Martin and me. They were only allowed to bring us sweets – no tobacco or anything else. We sat and had a fifteen-minute chat. I was glad to see a friendly face. I asked Anna, "Could you send a bunch of flowers to my mum and try to imitate my handwriting on a card?"

It seemed to work, because we were one month in that remand centre and when I got out my mother and father were none the wiser. I phoned them and told them lies, like: "Yeah, I haven't been writing lately because I have been so busy . . ."

Ashfield was quite different to the prisons I was later in. It was a very fearful regime. There was a comradeship, but nothing like the sort I was to find later on. Ashfield had a gang mentality. In other prisons it was more "them versus us", in that we would work with the prison officers to make it easy for everybody, but we would not take crap from them because we were all in the same boat. Compared to Ashfield, they were going to be a breeze.

Ashfield had two gangs: the Rastas and the Scots. The gang members looked out for one another. One day Martin and I were in the showers and these two Scots guys walked in. They were like mountain men. They said, "Get dried up and get out!" We all grabbed towels, lifted our clothes and got out. There was this one guy left behind whom they would not let out, and as we went up the corridor we could hear his screams. I found out later that the guy had been raped by two or three other prisoners, because they said he had interfered with children. I just walked past those Scots and always kept my head averted; I never looked at them. The same with the Rasta guys who would swagger along. I just deviated round them. We had heard rumours that other people got beaten up by warders but nothing happened to us. We knew the warders had the upper hand and complete control in Ashfield. At least they thought they did.

The week I was finally to get out on bail, we were standing in a line outside the canteen waiting to get our mail. The guy behind me got his letter and then the one behind him, then the warder stopped and presented the next letter which he had already read – they all were read before we were given them – and announced in a loud voice, "Smith, just to let you know, your mother's dead." There was absolute shock among all the prisoners at such callousness. I wasn't at all surprised to find out the following week, after we had got out on bail, that a riot had broken out. The prisoners had decided to club together in a way that they hadn't done before and they barricaded themselves into the canteen and didn't come out until certain things were addressed. I'm glad to say that Ashfield has been closed down for many years.

The lonely times in Ashfield were when I had plenty of time to think, especially in the quiet evenings when I would lie awake on my bed. Mum and dad and my brothers would go through my mind. I would think of Anna and what this would do to us. The news of the bust and the remand had been all over *The Surrey Chronicle* newspaper. Anna and her parents were respectable people. How could the relationship continue after this? I knew all this was going on outside the cell walls. Those were the sort of thoughts that went through my head, but at no time did I think: *Well, that is the end of drugs for me.* All I thought about was: *The next time, I will get it right. I will be more careful.* I still felt I was in control: I was not an addict. I was only into barbiturates. In short, there were no physical withdrawals to warn me about what was around the corner.

Chapter 13

Once we were out of Ashfield on bail, Martin and I couldn't wait to get back to the drugs, so we decided it would be business as usual. Big mistake. We slipped back into our roles as main dealers at The Three Fishes and we began shifting larger amounts of drugs for Nash. So we were being further drawn into his world.

Nash had a very easy way about him. He was very likable, and he never raised his voice. He would usually say something like, "D'you want to come over to the flat, smoke a few joints?" Our little gang socialised with his crowd. Whenever I went anywhere with Nash, people showed him reverence. I knew for some people it was because of the drugs, but he seemed to have a real hold on others. I tried to figure it out. Even though he kept the main part of the dealing away from his home patch, his flat was always full of people trying to get near him.

One day I asked him what was going on. He said he

was into a bit of astrology – worked out people's charts and signs. So Martin and I thought he could have a go with us. It seemed innocent enough. He asked me a few questions, like when I was born; and he plotted details into a chart. Then he told me he knew my favourite colour and number. They were all jokey things. Then he started to tell me about my personality.

Looking back on it all now, it was childish, but I didn't understand that this was Nash's way of screening us, bringing us into his inner circle. After some time, he told me he was into white witchcraft. His definition of a white witch was someone who used the occult for good, for healing. He was new age, I suppose. That satisfied some of my curiosity; but then he gave me a book called *Satan's Bible*. I quickly realised that Nash was actually into black magic.

Another time, I went to see him at his flat. I was let into the hall and heard some chanting going on. I opened the living room door and saw Nash and several others sitting around, chanting to strange music. I felt myself being lifted off the floor and thrown backwards down the hall. I began vomiting, and I had a real sense of evil around the place. I had never experienced anything like that before. Nash realised something was up. He came out into the hall and helped me up and into the bedroom. I asked him, "What was that? I am out of here." He said, "It was nothing, just lie there and it will be OK." I realised very quickly that this was not a place I wanted to be. When I got home, I told Martin all about it. He was sceptical, saying he didn't believe in black magic, but he became obsessed with the whole idea.

So, to satisfy his curiosity, we went back to Nash's one

night. We brought our friend Kev. We were only inside the place when Nash came over and touched Kev on the shoulder. Suddenly, Kev was lying flat on the sofa with his hands locked together. Nash even finished the experiment off, placing a book in Kev's hands. Kev's eyes were fixed. I'd never seen anything like it before in my life and I hope I never will again. Martin didn't need any more convincing. I decided I didn't want to have anything to do with it. Even though we would be around him, Martin and I began to distance ourselves mentally from Nash. I had felt he had a hold on me which I wanted to break away from. In later years, even though I had moved out of Nash's circle, somehow or other someone would get near me, and tell me that Nash sent his regards. Nothing unusual in that, but there was always something very frightening about it. The way it was, you could never feel free from Nash.

But I'm jumping ahead of myself. Before all of that, while we were out on bail, Martin and I had made a beeline for Nash's house. One afternoon we were hanging around, watching him get ready to go into the city to do a deal with one of his contacts. We sat in the room, chilling out, having a few joints and beers. We heard a key in the door, and in walked this little old lady – the woman we knew as "Mum". She was soaked to the skin, standing before us in the living room in a sopping mac and headscarf. In both hands she was carrying shopping bags, all full to the brim. She was having a hard job lifting them up onto the table, so I helped. The bags didn't feel like they were full of groceries; in fact they were full of dope and other drugs. Mum passed no remarks, took off her mac and headscarf, shook them out and sat down. Nash came over, gave her a peck on the cheek and asked her if she fancied a cuppa. She said "No thanks," that she was in a hurry and that he'd better get a move on if he was heading into London. It was just surreal. I felt like I was in the middle of a cosy domestic situation.

Even though we had been told Mum had no relationship with Nash, we would later find out that she was his lover, and they would go on to enjoy the sunny climes of Spain in their holiday home in later years. Mum had built up a nice little income for herself, working during the day for a telecommunications firm, and helping Nash with his drugs empire in her spare time. We later found out that she was very powerful in the drugs world; in fact, she was the driving force behind Nash. He was always under her guidance.

On that particular day Nash and Mum went off to get more drugs, while our gang – there were about twelve of us – stayed in the flat, with one of the bodyguards "baby-sitting" us. We didn't plan on the police arriving. We heard the thump, thump, thump: "Open up, it's the police!" None of us moved – we couldn't; we were all stoned out of our heads. One guy, Henry, turned around and took control of the situation: "Look, we are getting busted here, but it is only what we have in front of us, don't panic about it. There are twelve of us and there is only an ounce of dope. It's not going to be a big thing!" How wrong he was.

My first thought was that Martin and I were in big trouble, because we were out on bail, in the company of people who could be done for kilos of cannabis, and tens of thousands of amphetamine tablets, which would be big time. Bigger than us.

So what did we do? We got a fit of the giggles.

I got up to extinguish my half-joint. At this point the thumps stopped and the police came crashing in through the door. I dropped the joint behind a bookcase, thinking I'd get back to it later. The next thing I knew, my arm was pulled up behind my back until it touched my neck and I was in excruciating pain. A copper leaned over and said into my ear, "You are nicked, son." He made me pick up that half-joint from behind the bookcase with my other arm still locked.

I recognised this policeman; he was the same one I had come across during my first bust. He led Martin and me off to the police station, along with the rest. "You guys are fools," he said. "You have already got bail, you've seen what it's like being inside, and now you're out on bail and nicked again! What are you playing at?" I had no answer to that. I think he was just trying to help us out by letting us know how stupid we had been – trying to shake some sense into us. But we were living in our own little cocooned world – everybody wanted us, we were important, so why would we need to wake up to reality?

For the second time in 1972, I appeared in court again. This time it was in October at Surbiton and Sutton Crown Court. Now this was big time: I was up on two counts of possessing cannabis resin. I phoned dad and told him, and he got on a plane and came over to be with me. He even gave a letter to the court, vouching for his son's good character. In any event, it didn't turn out too bad for us. Nash's right-hand man turned Queen's Evidence on him, and Nash ended up being sentenced to seven years in prison. Martin and I just got two years' probation each. The prosecutors, in summing up the sentencing, said the police had thrown out a large net, and while they only caught one of the big fish – Nash – a lot of smaller fish had been reeled into the net at the same time. In other words, they had not been looking for small fry. It's not that they didn't want us to go to prison – they did – it was simply that we were up against Nash and he got the lion's share of the sentence.

My family were concerned about me and asked me to come home to Lisburn for a while to get my act together. So I went home with dad, and stayed there for a few weeks. They presumed I was working in some office and I never tried to tell them otherwise. Mum and dad tried their best over the years, tried to convince me on many occasions not to return to England – especially when I began to suffer from the beginnings of withdrawal. One of the side effects was called a "grand mal seizure". I had my first one in my parents' home around this time.

I was sitting on the sofa and suddenly I noticed a nervousness coming into my body and my mind. It was all a bit surreal. People who suffer from epilepsy would be able to identify with this – I had an awareness that something greater than me was taking over. It was to take several forms down through the years. This time I had a fit in which froth came out of my mouth. The danger was that I could swallow my tongue.

When mum and dad came back and saw me in this state, they sent for the doctor, who took me to one side and asked: "What have you been taking?" For once I was honest about the amount of drugs I had in my system and told him I got them because I was registered on the NHS. He told me I had been prescribed a "disgusting amount of drugs". This doctor then explained I could expect to have fits like this anytime if I suddenly stopped taking barbiturates. He suggested I try to get some help to come off the drugs. I thought he was off his trolley!

So when I had this seizure in my parents' house, I realised that this might be causing more trouble than it was worth, and I tried to avoid the drugs for a little while – for a matter of weeks, as it turned out. But then I went back to them. Like most addicts who do not admit they are addicts, I was convinced the seizure was a once-off and would never happen again. I was wrong.

Of course I had told mum and dad that I would not be taking any more drugs – whatever they needed to hear, I told them. They had tried their best to convince me on many occasions not to go back, especially after the seizure, when they made strenuous efforts, even resorting to bribery. Dad said, "We will buy you a car, if you would stay at home. Things aren't so bad here." But of course I would point to the Troubles and say to my parents, "There is nothing for me here." I think that half-convinced my dad. Even though he thought I might be on the edge of the drugs scene in the early years, he thought I would have enough intelligence to stay away from it. He gave me more credit than I was due. And when he looked at what was going on around him in Northern Ireland at that time, I think he was glad that his son was away from it all. Tom lived at home and worked in the same factory with Raymond. Raymond was married and had a daughter. Also, I think my parents felt that I had settled in England; I had a job there – they thought I was working in an office, but I was working as a barman in a pub in Kingston. At the time, I didn't realise my choice of profession was primarily dictated by my love for drugs – alcohol being one of them. I also had a place to live and I was old enough now to tell them what I was going to do, rather than ask their permission.

Of course, the draw of England and the drugs meant that it wasn't too long before I was back in London again, back in Kingston. By now Martin and Caroline's relationship had progressed to a more serious level. They moved in together. So it was time for me to move out of Manor Gate Road. I found a small flat in Sutton, Surrey. I just carried on as I had been, but I had no connection with Nash and I was not dealing any more. I'd had enough of that. I didn't like prison or the courts, and I didn't like the trouble the dealing caused.

Times began to get lonely. I was on my own. I didn't have the same number of friends I had had when I was dealing. Now, when I walked in the door of The Three Fishes I was just a punter like everyone else – no girls met me, nobody was hanging on my every word. It was a revelation to me – and this loneliness was frightening. I was still taking my own drugs, for personal use, mostly speed.

Anna and I were no longer together. Her father had said to her in the early part of our relationship, "One day you are going to end up sitting at the end of a bed with him sticking needles in his arm." Of course, at the time I thought that was ludicrous – that would never happen. Anyway, for one reason or another Anna and I broke up. I suppose the court cases proved too much, and with me going back and forth to Northern Ireland, we couldn't keep a long-distance relationship going. Besides, she took second place to the drugs; every woman did.

Things were falling apart around me. I had always felt I was not good enough for people to spend any great lengths of time with unless they were getting something from me. If I was selling some drugs, they would be there, but if I wasn't, they wouldn't. I don't think I ever felt I was really worth more than that, until I found God.

At this stage my daily drug taking had increased. The drugs were filling in the loneliness, or so I thought. I was working a week here, a month there in odd jobs. Then I would be back on the dole, then back working at something else again. I continued to get some very unpleasant side-effects from the drugs, like the fits, but of course this didn't put me off them.

Chapter 14

The next couple of years, 1973 and 1974, were to be very confusing and lonely for me. I'd often take a visit home to Lisburn. During one visit I met some of my old friends, who were into their dope, and they asked me if I could provide them with some good quality cannabis from London. They gave me the money and asked me to bring them back four ounces. As I still had some contacts, I agreed and got them what they wanted. One of the dealers gave me a little bit of LSD, asking, "Do you want to take that home with you, for your holiday?" I said, "Yeah, great!" I wrapped it up in a little piece of silver paper and tucked it inside my wallet. I never thought anything more about it.

On the Saturday night I flew back to Ireland, with the four ounces of cannabis packed in around my groin. When I got to the airport, the one piece of identification I had was my birth certificate, which was inside my wallet. I was carrying this certificate, because in those days you could get a cheaper flight if you were under twenty-two and could prove it. I went through the first check-in at the airport – no problem. I was about to board the plane when a Special Branch officer pulled me over and asked me to stand still while he searched me. He walked his hands straight up my legs, but finished just short of the cannabis. Then he asked, "Have you got any identification?" In my nervousness, I just handed him the wallet.

As he opened the wallet, he pulled out the certificate, looked at it, tucked it back in. And I could see, and he could see, that there was a little bit of silver paper pushing up from one of the pockets. He tapped it gently back into place with his forefinger, closed the wallet and said, "Sonny, only I'm after something much more important right now, I would turn you on your head and strip you naked. Now get on your plane and go."

I couldn't believe it. What I didn't know was that a man had actually bombed part of London that Saturday. Later, I saw the description and the artist's sketch in the paper – he had long hair and looked a little bit like yours truly. I was so thankful that I had got back safely.

As I was at home I decided to go to a peace festival in Antrim. The night before I had a strange dream: I was in a field and people were walking towards me. I woke up in a bit of a sweat. I went to the festival, sat in this field and listened to a few groups playing mediocre stuff. I was skinning up a joint, smoking it, passing it to my friends, when I saw four or five Drug Squad officers walking towards us, all from different angles. I threw the quarter ounce over my shoulder, into the grass. They rushed forward and grabbed me. I told myself that they could only get me for one joint, which they did. I was then out on police bail, staying at home waiting on this silly little charge to come up. After all it was only one joint; it couldn't be that serious, could it?

I decided that it might be a good idea if I went into some form of rehab. That would show the judge, when the time came, that I had done what I could to come off the drugs. I went to my GP and he referred me. So I did my first stint in rehab in a psychiatric ward in Antrim Hospital. I went in purely because I was on this drugs charge. I also thought it would be a great opportunity for me and that it would ensure I would walk out of court a free man.

I told the medics that I was desperately trying to get off drugs. I pretended to be on a higher amount of drugs, as the doctors had no idea of the level of amphetamines and barbiturates I was actually taking. That meant they gave me a higher dose than I usually took. So for the first week, I was pretty much stoned out of my head completely. Then I was ready for the treatment as, each day, they gave me decreasing amounts of these drugs. So by the time my court case came up, I was officially off drugs, but in reality I was still living on the level of drugs I was well used to. It worked a treat.

During those weeks in rehab I spent the time sitting around chatting with the other patients. Most of them were people who were having nervous breakdowns, due to drink or drugs problems. One guy was a long-termer. I called him Romy because he constantly paced up and down every night. He would only stop long enough for me to give him a cigarette and he never met my eyes. I could never get over that. I wrote a poem about him. I wrote a lot of poetry while I was in there. I thought it was a good way to express my feelings about the place.

There were all sorts of people there, from all walks of life. I met a teacher who had taken tranquillisers for years; when he went on holidays abroad and realised he couldn't get his drugs there, he went crazy. I also met a guy called Jack who was on the drugs scene at the same time as me. He seemed to be having a lot more difficulty than I was. He was in for genuine psychiatric reasons. Naively, I wondered how you could have such problems if you weren't taking drugs. But that was my first appearance in a psychiatric ward. I spent six weeks there.

I was young enough, and my experience of the police and courts was still fairly limited. I was sure I could not get sent down for something that I thought was a minor offence. When the court case was due in March 1974, dad accompanied me to Antrim Magistrates Court. The case before mine was a man accused of possessing rounds of .22 ammunition. This man received two months' imprisonment for possession of something that could kill people. I was up next for possession of one joint. The magistrate gave me four months. The perverted idea of justice!

I couldn't believe it. I turned pale; so did dad. The policeman turned to me in the dock and said, "Come on."

"Where are we going?"

"You're going down to Crumlin Road Prison."

"I don't think so, not for one joint."

I appealed it and was granted bail again. So I went back to England, and three months later travelled back for the appeal. I was given a two-year probation order, which couldn't be transferred to England – in other words, nothing. I flew back to England feeling quite justified that I had got off for just one joint. I never thought about what all of this must have been doing to mum and dad and my brothers. My only real concern by now was getting my drugs.

Chapter 15

The hippy generation had now woken up to the reality that it was not going to work. The beads and the bells were falling off from around our necks. Our hair remained long, the hearts remained strong. But at the end of the day I felt a real, personal disappointment for the first time in my life. I felt that the hippies had sold out, that we had a revolution but it had failed. The hippy ideal of peace, love and understanding was gone, and many were not prepared to think of others anymore. People just began to rip each other off.

However, when I look back on that time, I can see that society did change in a real way. It took two years for the hippy culture to be corrupted by the "plastic hippies", the drug dealers and the gangsters. I didn't count myself to be among the drug dealers as these were people solely in it for the money and profit. It made no difference to them whether they sold cannabis or stole TVs – they were just crooks. But in its wake, some good people had left their mark. Even though they had shaved their hair and now wore pinstriped suits and went to work in the bank, the world was never really the same. Even though these people went about their lives with the trappings of a new society around them, they had earned a unique type of respect.

But at the time the hippy dream was dying, it was a mirror of my life: some of my friendships, some of my hopes were dying. I had covered my emptiness with the hope of a hippy revolution. Now that was dead and the loneliness was back. I had a list of friends who had died of overdoses; friends like Lisa, Lorna, Dell. Other friends were disappearing from my life. Martin was practically married and I was no longer best buddies with him. Terry was involved in the Christian environment. So I was by myself.

I still didn't believe I was addicted. Sure, I was a user and an abuser but certainly not an addict. I thought addicts were people who stuck needles in their arms and I would never do that. The fact that several doctors were still prescribing me free drugs on the NHS actually reassured me that I did not have a serious problem. I thought I might have a slight problem, but it was not even something the doctors were worried about, so why should I?

When I wasn't in Lisburn I was back living in Kingston-upon-Thames. I was not dealing; I was just existing on my drugs. I took a handful in the morning, along with some alcohol, and got on with things. I wasn't working much, but I had the dole money and my steady prescriptions from the doctor. I ended up spending time with different people, the odd time living in different squats.

It wasn't all bad. I was like many other people who used the dole money to pay their rent. Sometimes I got a bit of spare money from doing odd jobs but that went on beer and drugs. A few friends from the early days were still around. One of them was Kathy.

I had first been introduced to Kathy in the romantic setting of a crowded pub, back in 1972. I was there one night drinking and taking drugs with some friends. She was very thin and had piercing green eyes and curly brown hair. I liked her because she had a wicked sense of humour. We came to spend a bit of time together. We were more friends than boyfriend and girlfriend. We did spend a few nights together, but this was not unusual in those days – friends slept together, it wasn't a big thing. In those years, it was sometimes difficult to know the difference between a serious relationship and a good friendship. Kathy became both to me. I don't think either of us would ever have said it was love; it was just hippy love, or the dying embers of the hippy dream.

As the years passed, we would see less and less of each other. I was getting deeper into drugs, and Kathy was getting into alcohol. When we did team up for a while it was usually because all our other friends had moved on or out of the scene completely. Our chance encounters were like two lame ducks trying to help each other out.

But back to the story. Around this time, I voluntarily checked myself into another psychiatric hospital, this one in Surrey. I was making some sort of effort to get off the drugs. In truth I knew I'd get more drugs there. When Terry came to visit me, I first began to realise just how serious my drug problem was. He had become a Christian a few years before. My other friend, Martin could not understand why I was bothering to sign myself into these places. He had been to visit and had said, "Come on out for a pint." But I did not want to stay out. The day Terry came to visit me, I was waiting in the corridor for him. I could see him walking towards me – and that's when I had a grand mal seizure. That was the first in a long, long time.

I began to feel very light-headed; a very surreal feeling came over me and I felt myself drifting, back, back, back. The next thing, I blacked out. My tongue went back in my mouth, the froth came out and my whole body twitched and shook. I was having this seizure because I was withdrawing from barbiturates. So there was Terry looking down the corridor at me in this state, having something like an epileptic seizure in front of everybody in the corridor of the hospital. Terry later told me that they held me steady for a moment or two and then lifted me up, one on each leg and arm, brought me into a room, put me on the bed and left me there.

I remember reading about that place years later in the paper. It wasn't good. I only stayed there for four weeks and I got out. I always found that if I was going to have any chance of staying off drugs, the only place I could do it was home. That was because of the support of my parents and my brothers. It was the only time I found relative peace.

So once again I came home to Lisburn because I thought

things were not working out in London. I had come to my senses – or so I thought – and decided to get off the drugs. I became respectable. I got a job in Lisburn, working in the same factory as my two brothers. Each day I got up, went to work and weaned myself down off the drugs. I was clean and I worked hard – but I also drank hard. I didn't realise that I was replacing one drug with another. The emptiness, that horrible feeling, which was even more prevalent inside me, demanded more and more liquor. I had to fill that bottomless void.

The factory produced steel bins. I did a bit of labouring and was making good money. My parents were relieved that I seemed to have found myself, that I had settled down at home, that I was living a routine regular life. While working in the factory I met a few ordinary nine-to-five guys and I started drinking heavily with them after work. This went on for about a year. During this time, the Troubles were still raging. You had to be careful where you went to drink and whom you went with. A lot of the time I found myself drinking in Catholic bars. There was always an awareness that you could be targeted. It was a nightmare of a time – but we got through it by drinking and working hard.

Soon I was drinking two or three times a day. This would consist of large amounts of booze, anything from vodka and whiskey to cider and anything else in between. I was also putting on a lot of weight. One day I walked past a shop window and saw myself reflected back. There I stood, half drunk, in a pair of overalls, with a huge beer belly. And I thought, you know, this is crap. I was better off before. So I made my way straight down to the

Lisburn Health Centre and I sat with tears in my eyes and told a doctor who I knew well, that really I couldn't go on with the straight life. The doctor, foolishly or not, gave me a prescription for amphetamines; after all, I was still a registered drug user. So I was back running on the hamster wheel again.

When Kathy was your friend, she was your friend for life. So it came as no big surprise to me when in 1975 she wrote to me. She said she had been pregnant and that she had had a baby girl. She named her Tracey. Kathy thought I might be the father and asked me would I like to come over and spend some time with her. Her letter was a plea; she needed company. I was later to find out that Kathy had contacted quite a few guys because she wasn't sure whose baby she was carrying. But she presented me with an attractive offer. I was back on speed and the drugs were taking over my ability to work. I knew I was not going to want to work in the factory for much longer. I was also fed up living at home with my parents. I needed my own space.

I knew Kathy was set up; she had inherited a house in Wales from her uncle, in a place called Builth Wells. I thought: *This is good.* Kathy was over there with the child, and this might be a good way to get back into the old days and into some semblance of a hippy life. After all, I was a registered addict and I could get speed in Wales as well as in Northern Ireland.

Decision made, I packed my bags and told my mum and dad that I was thinking of getting married. It might have seemed out of the blue, but Kathy and I had both seen many of our friends leaving the hippy dream behind, taking on responsibilities, getting married and settling down. Of course, we were two lonely friends floating around in this new reality. We felt the loneliness, we felt detached from our past. We needed to hang onto something. That something was each other. We had this weird idea that if we got married, it would somehow make us different, more responsible, and in a way more secure in our feelings towards each other.

My parents reacted positively to the news that I might be about to tie the knot. They wished us well, crossed their fingers and hoped for the best. Kathy met me at the airport in a happy drunken state. She was pretty heavily into the drink by this stage. She took me to her parents' home in Staines, near Walton-on-Thames, just outside the Greater London area. That was when I first set eyes on little Tracey – a cute little girl, with blonde hair and blue eyes. I immediately felt very protective of both Kathy and Tracey, so I took on the responsibility of fatherhood at the age of twenty-one. Of course, there was only one other thing to do, to make the dream turn into a reality, and that was the small matter of proposing.

We stayed with Kathy's parents in Staines. We lived in the top floor of their large house. So we had space to ourselves and also the use of the kitchen. One morning I was woken to the sound of Kathy banging cupboard doors. Tracey was asleep in her cot and Kathy's parents were away for the day. I strolled down to the kitchen, peered around the corner and saw Kathy rummaging through the cupboards for breakfast bowls. I noticed a couple of bottles of wine on the table; one of them was half empty. I went over, picked it up and took a drink.

"Mornin'," I said, giving Kathy a peck on the cheek.

"Mornin'. Would you like some breakfast?"

"Sure – what have we?"

"Cornflakes."

"Do grand."

We both sat down to eat. We looked at the bowls of cornflakes in front of us. "Where's the milk?" I asked.

"Forgot to get some."

"Never mind."

Kathy then lifted the bottle and poured the wine onto her cereal.

"Want to get married?" I asked.

"Yeah, cool."

I said I'd phone the Registry Office and, if they had a vacancy on my birthday, 3 May, then we would get married. I never thought Staines would have a vacancy, but they did.

Kathy's parents wanted to organise the reception. Her mother was constantly on the phone ringing up her relations, getting it all sorted out. I think her parents were reservedly glad to think that their daughter was putting some stability into her life.

The following week I stood before the registrar in Staines Registry Office, in my best suit, wearing a big carnation, sober as I could be. Kathy looked like she was on for making a go of things. Martin was my best man and passed over the rings at the required time. It was all very surreal. Half the room was full of our mates with their long hair while the other, the middle class gentry, were all in their Sunday best. The reception was in a local pub.

Kathy's dad spent most of it sitting up at the bar, looking reproachfully down at all our lot, as he downed the odd whiskey. The wedding party was filling up the function room and the old hippies were making an impression.

A friend of ours, Mark, was at his dramatic best. He arrived into the room and made a big deal about introducing his new Swedish girlfriend to Kathy's male cousins. Then, just like the parting of the waves, he gestured with his arm and the crowd moved away. Mark was wearing a big black cape, tied very theatrically at the neck with a huge bow. He practically floated up to us at the bar, put his hand inside his cape, and pulled out an ounce of dope, roughly wrapped in wedding paper. Kathy and I got into it straight away, and our party moved out into the beer garden, where we hippies were more at home sitting on the grass, chilling.

At that time I still didn't realise that my love for drugs was greater than any love I could have had for Kathy. Likewise, her love for alcohol was greater than any love she could have had for me.

Settling into what we thought was married life, Kathy, Tracey and I travelled as a family up to Wales. We stayed in for a few weeks, but I was never really happy with it all. Builth Wells was not the centre of the universe for me. The local pub was about all the excitement there was, along with a handful of hippies. A few of the old crowd from London came to stay with us the odd weekend, but that only increased the longing in me to get back to Kingston, to The Three Fishes, and to where the drugs were more plentiful.

So I said goodbye to Kathy and little Tracey and headed off. Kathy and the baby followed me later on and we spent a bit of time staying in her parents' house. Then we decided to take a trip back to Builth Wells, but what we didn't know was that a girl called Jane, a girlfriend of my old friend Paul Arrowsmith, had invited some people into the house while we were away. These guys had actually decided that they would concoct a homemade bomb. I think it was made of fertiliser or something, and they put it, of all places, in the hot press. The thing exploded. When we arrived back at Kathy's house in Wales, the police were all over the place. So you can imagine how I felt, in the middle of Wales with a Northern Ireland accent. There was, however, no suspicion that Kathy or I were involved. We had been down the south of England at the time.

I took this as a cue to get back to Kingston for a time. I teamed up again with Martin. Then Kathy and I moved back in with her folks and began playing at being married grown-ups. Six months into our domestic set-up, I was working, trying to be responsible. I came in the door after my first day at work. Kathy was lying unconscious on the floor; she was drunk. Her dad was looking after Tracey.

That was just one scene out of a marriage that never really had a chance. Our relationship as man and wife lasted a total of six months. It failed because we were living as two single people – neither one of us willing to give up the freedom of our drugged lifestyle. We had no real sense of responsibility. Tracey was the one in the middle of all this who was suffering. We couldn't even be responsible for ourselves, so how could we be responsible for her? We would take it in turns each day to act as responsible parents for our baby. That's how immature we were. We were lucky we had Kathy's parents to fall back on. In the end we knew we couldn't hack it as man and wife. It wasn't fair on anyone.

Kathy and I separated with no hard feelings; we were just better at being friends than husband and wife. We were just muckers, drinking partners, dope takers – but we were never really serious. I never felt sad about it all, and Kathy to this day still remains a friend, as does Tracey. Even though I had become a father to Tracey her grandparents helped bring her up, along with Kathy, and they did a very fine job of it.

Chapter 16

So, I went back to living in Kingston. I got to know an English guy called John Gayle, and I ended up staying in his house. My drug-dealing days were long over, but my addiction – which I was still denying – was in full flow. The days of larking about, experimenting with drugs had gone and by then it was simply about getting my supply from the doctor and adding it to other supplies. One of the ways I supplemented my stash was by forging prescriptions.

One time I broke into a doctor's surgery in Surrey to steal a prescription pad. I had gone to see the doctor earlier that day. I knew before I went that there wasn't much chance that he would give me the drugs I wanted. I told him I was a registered addict but he refused to give me anything worth talking about. Instead he gave me some anti-depressants, which I laughed at. I decided that if he was not going to write me a prescription, then I would write it. So on the way out of his waiting room, I took time to lift the latch on one of the windows and push it slightly over. I returned later that night, climbed in through the window, went into his surgery and lifted out a prescription pad and some sick notes. I have no idea why I took the sick notes, because I was not working at the time. I just thought: *I may as well lift them.*

This was my first attempt at writing prescriptions and I was doing it from memory. I latched on to a Latin word, *mitte*, which you find on nearly every prescription form. It means "amount" or "number". But a little bit of Latin went a long way for me. I practised for some time until I got a few prescriptions written out to my satisfaction. I just sat in the house with John and wrote the prescription and the doctor's signature out a few times until it all looked right. As long as I knew how to spell, I thought, I was in with a chance.

Next, I had to test it out. The first thing I did was to take it to a local chemist and hand him the prescription. He looked at me oddly. I panicked, because I thought he was surprised at the amount! But no, he was surprised at my accent. It turned out he was originally from Northern Ireland. So there we were having a chat about the old sod back home, and all the time I was thinking: *Flipping brilliant, this guy is actually going to do this!* He gave me the huge quantities of amphetamines and barbiturates I had applied for.

This was great; I had entered a new phase of my drug-taking life as a forger. I got a great buzz from it and was excited to think that I was not only getting the drugs that I wanted but I was able to put any amount down. It was another step deeper into my love affair with drugs.

I got so good at it that over the next few weeks, I hit different chemists at different times. Nobody batted an eyelid. It seemed I was infallible.

I had a friend called Marvin and one night we were in his flat scoring some dope. I started to run low on my pills. I said, "Where can we go to get a prescription filled right now?" It was the middle of the night. After much deliberation we thought, why don't we try the airport? So we drove up to Heathrow Airport. Marvin and his girlfriend sat outside in the car. I went in to Terminal One and over to the all-night chemist shop. The police were patrolling around the whole time, especially in this terminal, because this was where the Irish usually met. Undeterred, I went to the pharmacist and handed him a prescription note. He took it and went into the back of the shop. I waited, tapping my feet. Minutes passed. He seemed to be taking a little bit too long. I was beginning to panic, thinking that if he didn't come out soon with the pills, I would have to get out of there. I was about to run when he came back to the counter. He said, "Look I'm really sorry about this . . ." – my heart missed a beat – ". . . but I haven't enough Dexedrine here. I am going to have to go over to Terminal Two to get some more."

So, after locking up his shop, off this gentleman went. (He really was a gentleman; he was dressed in a suit, was in his sixties and was a very helpful chap.) He hot-footed it the whole way over to Terminal Two and came back with my speed. When he handed me those tablets I remember saying, "Only it wouldn't be legal, I would love to give you a tip. Thanks for your help."

For me, nothing was an inconvenience when it came to

getting drugs. I would have done almost anything for them, and wouldn't have thought twice about hurting others along the way. Although at the time, I would not have realised what I was doing.

On a new high with my great success as a forger, I then made the big mistake that everybody should watch out for: I got cocky. It's never a good idea to crap in your own nest. As I was living in Kingston, I filled my normal prescription there and, being lazy one Saturday, I went into the same chemist shop that I had used months before. It wasn't my regular one, but I had used it. I handed over a prescription with a different name on it and they hit the alarm bell. Marvin was waiting outside in the car. I ran out of the shop, hopped in the car and asked Marvin to drive me into Kingston town. We got to the centre of Kingston and I jumped out of the car. By now the police were on my tail. I went through a big store to lose them. I then got a bus going over the bridge in Kingston and went back to John's house.

Later that night, as I was sitting there, the police arrived. I had a large amount of barbiturates and some LSD in my duffle-coat pockets. The coat was hanging in the hall. Now I was being arrested in John's house. The police told me I had to come over to the station. It was just across the road, very convenient, but it was quite a chilly night. I deliberately went to walk out without my coat, but John, thinking he was being caring, said, "Here man, put your coat on before you freeze." So unfortunately there was no hope of me getting out of this one!

I was brought into the CID room. In the interview the

guy was getting the relevant confession out of me: yes, I did try to forge prescriptions; yes, those were barbiturates in my pocket; and yes, that was LSD. Then he did a very unusual thing: he got up from the desk, leaving the drugs there, and he went next door to a colleague. I could hear them talking and it crossed my mind that if I were to grab the drugs and swallow them, they would have no evidence. I even thought: *Well, at least if I took a few, then I would be stoned, and I could quite enjoy the rest of my arrest.*

I was just about to do it, when I saw a blackened window to my right. Was he behind it? I didn't know, but to test it out I said out loud, "If you think I am going to grab these while you are out of the room, then you are mistaken." At that moment he rushed back into the room, nearly tripping over himself.

So I had to take my chances at Kingston Magistrates Court. I was still quite stoned out of my mind when I was in the dock. I was not allowed bail. Because I was over twenty-one years of age, I qualified to see the inside of a real prison for the first time. They sent me off to Brixton for an overnight stay.

I was brought into prison and went through reception. I was a bit lippy to the prison warders, so they man-handled me and pushed me up the steps. It was late at night and they just threw me into the cell, into the darkness. As I hit the far wall of the cell I heard a Northern Ireland accent asking, "You all right there?" I couldn't believe it – here was somebody from home, in the same cell as me. Even stranger than fiction, this guy turned out to be my brother Raymond's best friend's brother. We had a great night, spent it chatting about the wonderful things of home and how we would have loved to be there right then. My cellmate told me the bizarre story of how he had ended up inside. He had got drunk and, instead of walking home, had decided to take a lift off a lorry driver. This lorry unfortunately then became involved in a high-speed police chase. It crashed and unloaded its cargo all over the motorway. It turned out it had been filled with thousands of contraband cigarettes!

The next day, I was up in Kingston Court again and they gave me bail. I had received a total of three months suspended for two years, for stealing the prescription pad, passing it, and for having the drugs on me. It was January 1976 – what a great start to the year! That was my first, tiniest experience of "real" prison. But as bad as it was, it still wasn't going to be enough to put me off.

Chapter 17

We had been very busy at the end of 1975. As I said, by now Martin was back on the scene. He had worked hard at being Mr Sensible, living with Caroline, and keeping down a job. However, every so often, the terrible duo would reunite. One morning, we met up with John Gayle. We were sitting in his car, drinking and chatting, when an idea came to me, and I asked them: "Why don't we have a go at trying to rob somewhere?" We had done almost everything else but we'd never done that before. So we talked it over and finally decided: "Why not?"

We drove to Southall. There was a very big immigrant population there, mostly Pakistanis and Indians, so of course we stood out like big sore thumbs – three white guys sitting in a red Ford Escort. We spotted a little newsagents and decided we'd start our robbing career there. I hid a wheel brace inside my duffle coat and we went in. There was a little elderly Indian lady behind the counter. John shouted, "Open the till!" I slammed the wheel brace down on the counter. The woman was terrified and opened the till straight away and we each grabbed a handful of money. Martin was the wheelman, so he sat in the car with the engine running. We ran out, got into the car and drove further into Southall. We looked at the money – it wasn't very much, but it was only our first time.

Our idea was to use the money to buy drink. Then we thought, why not rob an off-licence, kill two birds with one stone? We picked an off-licence that was very busy. We reckoned that this store would have bags of money. We sat outside in the car watching, waiting until there was a slack period. Finally, there were no customers, and we could just see one Pakistani guy behind the counter. So in we went. John put a bottle of wine on the counter, the guy rang the till and the till sprang open. At the sound, I slammed the wheel brace down and shouted, "Leave it open!" The guy started talking very fast and suddenly seven others came running out of a room at the back.

Well, we were out of there so fast! I sprinted up the street with these guys chasing me. I looked over my shoulder and saw that John was already on the ground, getting kicked. I dropped the wheel brace. Martin had the car moving slowly away with the door open. I jumped in and yelled, "Go! Go!" John was still lying on the ground being kicked as we drove off. Suddenly, with the car door half-open, the wheel brace came flying and hit me in the ribs, cracking one. As we moved up another gear, I looked round and saw the guys picking it up and throwing it again. That's when it came through the windscreen.

I was screaming, "Marty, take me to Heathrow! I want to go home, this is not fun anymore."

"No. Let's get back to my flat. We will talk it over."

"OK, but I'm going home. This is bad news, man."

We got back to Martin's flat, which was above a chemist shop, ironically. The staircase up to the flat was really narrow, but we were running so fast that we scrambled up it. No sooner were we in than I collapsed into a chair, nursing my ribs. Martin and I were both smoking cigarettes, wondering what to do next, when we heard a familiar thump-thump on the stairs, followed by a hammering on the door:

"Armed police – do not move!"

Martin got up and calmly opened the door. He coolly looked at the heavy-duty policeman and said, in a tone rather too relaxed for my liking, "OK, calm down, man! It's not *The Italian Job*."

We were up before the judge at Knightsbridge Crown Court in January 1976 for a preliminary hearing. The judge was dressed in bright red with the required wig. I couldn't keep my eyes off the ermine he was wearing and he had his wee gavel in front of him. All the barristers were wearing black capes and were talking about me, saying things like, "under the present circumstances". It was kind of weird; I didn't understand what was going on.

I was looking at two years here, for robbery and attempted robbery. Bail was set at something over a couple of thousand pounds, so the authorities were viewing this very seriously. Martin and John got out on bail because they had family there to stand by them. I hadn't told my parents what had happened. I didn't want them to find out, because of the shame it would bring on them.

I didn't even apply for bail. I knew I was going down. I thought that I was going to get some sort of time, so I might as well do as much of it as I could on remand. I had heard that things were a lot more relaxed for remand prisoners; at least, that was my logical thinking. So my defence lawyers said, "While we wouldn't apply for bail at this point, we may later on." I was remanded in custody for a month to Brixton Prison. Under the remand system, you appear before the judge every month until you either have your case heard or you are granted bail. I would be brought back to the court on four future dates, and my remand would last a total of four months.

Chapter 18

After that first court appearance, I was put into a court cell; there were about twenty others in the cells as well, all waiting to be taken to Brixton. After a while, some of us were taken out of the cells and put into a police van, which had about twelve little cubicles or cells with doors in it. They were called "boxes" – they were really narrow and I just had enough room to stand up inside. The doors closed and locked. Everyone had their own individual little windows, so I could see through the "slots" to the outside whizzing past, but that was about it. It was a very strange experience – I felt totally isolated and hemmed into this upright coffin. The homesickness and the isolation came flooding back. A feeling of helplessness, of losing control, overpowered me.

I glanced up through the slot and saw something that I had only ever seen in films or on the news. Approaching Brixton is just like it is in the movies. That famous old-fashioned entrance appeared bit by bit – the Victorian archway that straddles the main entrance to Brixton prison.

The van drove under this famous arch and in through the main doors. The box stopped moving. The gates were locked. There was a lot of shouting going on – "Number 52, 53!" – it went on and on. Prison officers signed papers and then the huge wooden entrance door opened. I proceeded in my box into the courtyard of Brixton Prison.

I was unlocked from my upright coffin and brought out of the van in handcuffs, out into the light of day. I looked around me and saw six others who had been holed up in their own little cells in the same van. The first thing that struck me was the shouting. The prisoners were screaming down at us, "Welcome to Brixton!" It was black prison humour and, in a funny way, it relaxed my nerves. I was thinking: *Well, it can't be that bad, if these guys can shout out of their cell windows and get away with it.* That sort of thing would never have happened in Ashfield.

We went into the reception area. It was different to Ashfield. Here we were all kept together, in the communal room, while the paperwork was processed. The guards were not shouting or bawling at me. Of course, they didn't say "please"! While we were sitting there, we all started to talk about what we were in for – we were all in the same boat. One guy seemed to be on a bit of a high, going on about a major drugs bust. My ears pricked up. He had long hair; he was one of our wider gang. We were chatting away and he kept saying how the Drug Squad were brutal. I didn't think he was really believed because he kept claiming that they had tortured him during the couple of days he was in the police station. One of the prisoners said, "That is a load of crap." And he replied, "Is it?" He took his boots and socks off. He said, "Look at my feet. They burned them with cigarette butts." And sure enough, on the soles of his feet were all these cigarette burns. I was thinking: *Haven't I been lucky?*

There was also a huge guy there shouting very loudly at the prison officers: "Why am I not getting special treatment? I am a diplomat." We all heard this and laughed at it, but later that week we found out that he was in fact under the diplomatic service of some African country. He was given proper meals which were brought into the prison and he was also given some wine. He obviously had pull that the rest of us didn't have.

Then it was time for me to become acquainted with my cell. My old friends, the three plastic potties, the fashion accessories of the modern cell, were there to greet me. There was not much of a difference between the cell at Ashfield and the one in Brixton – except, perhaps, that it was a lighter shade of gray!

The big difference, however, was that Brixton was not run in a military fashion. There was a bit more of a sense of comradeship amongst the men. Everybody inside had the same idea – that we would not let the screws get us down. I met many characters in there. An Italian guy, Giovanni, cut everybody's hair. I decided to get rid of my flowing locks and he cut them off for me. I was a bit apprehensive, but he did a great job. I've never had a haircut like it since. He would even style it for my remand court appearances. We paid him in tobacco.

During my time on remand, every couple of weeks I would be returned to court for bail hearings. There was this particular cop who had led the team into the flat on the day or our arrest. He was part of the investigation and he would come down to the cell below the court on those occasions. He would get the guard to pull back the peephole and he'd taunt me, saying things like, "Alright sunshine, going for your tea soon, going for your tea soon!" In other words, it wouldn't be long until I would get sent down. And he would torment me!

So one week I was going up for bail again, knowing I wouldn't get it. The guard pulled back the peephole and there the cop was with his wee smile and his, "Not be long, sunshine, now. Not be long, sunshine, going for your tea." But I was waiting on him this time. I was stretched out on the bunk bed in the cell and I said, "Well, to tell you the truth, you know, I'm a lot better off than you are." I was still lippy.

He said, "What d'ya mean?"

"Well, you see, suppose I come up before the judge and I get two years?"

"Oh, you will, sunshine, you will."

"But when that two years is over, I'll have no need to worry anymore. But you, you've got a real reason to worry."

"What's that?"

"Haven't you noticed?" I said, laying on the accent a bit thicker, "I'm from Northern Ireland. One day you are going to be walking down the street, it may be late in the evening, and somebody's going to take you up an alleyway and take you out."

All lies, of course, but he went absolutely nuts.

"Open this door up!"

The screws were so frightened of his temper that they wouldn't let him into the cell, and I just sat and laughed at him. It was all a big wind-up, a joke to me, of course, because I had never been involved in anything like that. But what I said had hit him on a sore spot.

My mainstay drugs in Brixton, my cigarettes, were most important. I was determined to do my time as best I could without the other drugs in my system. In remand in the men's prison, I found out that I could get two hundred cigarettes or four ounces of tobacco sent to me every week. I had to get my head around the fact that this was to be my only drug.

Now that I was in a real prison, I knew I was going to be there for a long time. It was not like in Ashfield, where I didn't tell my parents. Of course, I sent a letter off right away to mum and dad, letting them know where I was and what I was in for, and asking for the necessities that I needed. I wasn't aware at the time how they took the news, but I found a sympathetic pair of ears in my brother Tom. Ever the realist, he asked about how I was getting on and what I needed, and his response was that my mum and dad would send something over every week.

True to their word, they would pack a large cardboard box, filling it with cookies, sweets and two hundred cigarettes, as well as local newspapers from home – everything I could possibly need to survive. They even sent me money to buy a radio so I would have something to listen to in the evenings. This box would arrive every week without fail. My parents used to take it down to Dunmurry Post Office, which was a little place some distance from the main town of Lisburn, so that no one would see that they were posting this huge box to their son in Brixton Prison. The irony was that the prison officer who would deliver it to me was from Derry. I'm sure he knew what was happening but he never made any comments about it.

Day to day, it was all routine. I woke up every morning at six o'clock to the sound of a bang on the cell door. The warders would walk past the cells, dragging their sticks along the iron. I'd hear, "Slop out! Slop out! Slop out!" I would get moving, make the bed – I didn't have to make it military fashion, just straighten it. If it looked OK, it would pass. At about half past six, the warders would open the cell doors.

I would go get breakfast. I had to walk down to the canteen, four floors down. My breakfast would be presented to me on a cold metallic tray. I got whatever everybody else was having for breakfast that morning – usually watery scrambled eggs. I could have about seven pieces of bread but only a tiny knob of butter; I'd get a mug of tea but no sugar. It was all designed like that. I would bring the breakfast back to my cell and the doors would be locked. I would sit on my bunk with plastic knives and forks but a metallic tray, the kind you could have bashed somebody over the head with.

Later on I would listen to the radio or have a chat with my mates. The other prisoners on my wing became my mates, even though on the outside I would probably have had nothing in common with some of them. I knew I had to live alongside these guys, so it was best that I got on with them. We filled up the empty hours swapping our life stories, talking about family, football, anything. Doing something concrete with my free time was very important, especially if I wanted to keep my mind occupied and have a chance of surviving. So when I wasn't making conversation, I would read, play chess, draughts, Scrabble, anything I could get my hands on.

At eleven o'clock each morning, we would have a half hour of exercise, which involved the stimulating walk around the prison yard! The first time I went out for this breath of air I stood for a few minutes in the centre and looked over the high prison wall and the barbed wire. I could see a church spire in the distance, which reminded me of a church in Lisburn. I got a pang of homesickness. It was just a spire, a piece of a building, but it meant a lot to me. I turned around to talk to the guy beside me, pointed at it and said, "That reminds me of home."

Lunch was followed by listening to the radio, reading and passing the afternoon as best I could. Then it was the same for my tea, and I'd get another half hour for what the authorities would term "association". This was the time in the evening when all the prisoners could get together, have a chat and play a game of pool. There were twenty people at any one time eagerly waiting behind the two playing pool, so the chances were you would never get a game. After that, it was lights out and I slept until the next morning.

That was my eventful day.

One night, chatting with the other prisoners, I asked their opinions: would I get the minimum two-year sentence even though I was doing remand? They all thought I would still get the two years. In my mind this had been confirmed by "the experts". So I knew that I would be in prison for a long time and I was going to have to get used to it. The thought of taking drugs to help me through it was alien to me, though. The only way that I could handle doing this kind of time was to stay off drugs. So I deliberately chose not to ask for medical help when I felt at a low ebb, and there were many such times.

I shared my cell with a guy called Bill Darby. Small and wiry, he was a City gent who worked for a big computer company, had worn pin-striped suits, and worked hard. He was the most unlikely character for it, but he was in for GBH. It turned out that he had been away on business as usual, but decided to collect his son from school and come home early to surprise the wife. They were going to celebrate twenty years of marriage. But when he came home, he found his wife in bed with his best friend. He went mad and hit the guy and in the process his wife was injured.

This middle-class gent told me how, before that, he had been trying to get to the top in his career. He was mortgaged to the hilt. He would have had a few beers at the weekends but never got drunk. He told me that it seemed like a red mist had come over him that day and he had just gone for it. All his friends disowned him after he cracked up like that. One of his friends took the trouble to write to him in prison to tell him what a scoundrel he was.

Brothers in arms: Tom, Raymond and me

Me as a young lad, full of hope

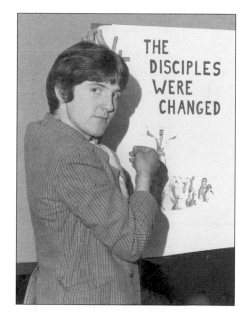

As a teenager in the local youth group

Tonagh Estate in Lisburn around 1967

Dad on right with his boss, Prime Minister of Northern
Ireland, Terence O'Neill

The Hippy
Me at 19

In the back garden in Lisburn, early 1970s

Prepared for court – Chester, England in the early 1970s

With Mum and little Emma outside the cottage
at Lagham Manor

Family Christmas, including Tom (with party hat)

Mum and Dad in the garden of our old home in Lisburn

Me in Lisburn, late 1970s

Lisburn, late 1970s

Mum on her 89th Birthday!

Hilary and I on our Wedding Day in 1997

The kids:
Rachel, Jonathan and Matthew

The evidence –
me with my
case of "drugs"

Speaking to a group of school children about the dangers of drugs

I kept Bill supplied in cigarettes. We got on well, we enjoyed each other's company and we swapped stories about our two completely different lives. So when after two months I was told I was being moved to Pentonville Prison to continue with my remand, Bill asked them if we could keep sharing as cellmates in the new place, and they agreed. I was glad because I didn't want to lose my friend. It was easy to do my time with him. He was refreshing to be with, because he was so different to me, so unlike all my friends on the outside.

Chapter 19

Because of overcrowding, remand prisoners only ever stayed in Brixton Prison for about two months; after that they were moved to Pentonville, on the other side of London. So Bill and I were bussed in the meat wagon to Pentonville, along with all the other remand prisoners. Being first-timers in a "grown-up" prison, we had no idea what we were going to. The others did, but didn't say much. We arrived and the routine in reception was the same as at Brixton. The first thing I noticed when we came out of reception was two warders standing in the middle of the basement floor, laughing at two cockroaches racing each other up the tiled wall. It was a bit surreal.

Like Brixton, Pentonville was a Victorian prison, but it was much dirtier. During "slop-out" in the morning, the place stank. It was like living in a cesspit compared to Brixton. I found the prison warders less friendly too. But otherwise, the regime was much the same as in Brixton –

half an hour of exercise, "slop out, slop in", "lock up, lock out".

Being in prison, especially so far away from home, it is hard to think that there'd be anything but heartache, but that was just not the case. I found out that there was a guy up the corridor from me who was a great artist. His name was Theo, and he was so good that the Prison Governor had commissioned him to paint a portrait of him. Theo may have been a really good artist, but he was also a bit of a con artist. He was doing time for fraud. He used to go into restaurants in Soho with a false identity card, pretending he was a health inspector. He would run his fingers through a layer of dust and say, "I'm going to have to do you." The owners would look alarmed. Then Theo would follow it on by saying, "But I am open to a bribe."

There was plenty of free access in Pentonville. The cell doors were left open for periods in the day so we could walk in and out of each other's cells. During a recreation period I went to visit Theo in his cell. He had a cell to himself, probably a favour from the Governor because he liked his portrait. Theo had long hair, but he kept it short by tying it back neatly. I watched at the cell door as this tall skinny guy began dabbing reds and blues onto this battered old canvas. He was lost in his painting.

It was almost a sin to break through his trance, so I shuffled around a bit until the sound reached his ears. He turned around.

"I was just wondering," I began, "if I got a photo, would you be able to do anything with it?"

"Certainly."

"What would you do a painting for?"

"For a couple of ounces of tobacco." It was for next to nothing really, but was big money in prison.

So I wrote to my mum. Trying to pour some healing oil over the troubled waters, I told her about Theo. I asked her to send me over a small photo of Joanne, my brother Raymond's daughter. Mum sent back a tiny school photograph – about one inch square. I thought, *This is not going to work*. I didn't think Theo would be able to do anything with it. But I took it to him anyway and gave him his tobacco.

For the next few days I hovered around his cell door, trying to get a glimpse over his shoulder to see what was happening. I was really looking forward to seeing the portrait. When you have nothing else to think about or to look forward to in prison, something as simple as a guy painting a portrait for you becomes your whole world.

The day it was finished, I eagerly went over to Theo's cell. I saw it propped up between the bunk and the brick wall, with the afternoon sun trailing over it. There was my niece, looking warm and happy, immersed in these wonderful colours. And she was free and had her whole life in front of her. I stood there, not knowing what to say. Theo had created something more magical than a simple painting. He had created hope and, strangely, tied me more closely to my mum and dad as I felt pangs of homesickness sweep over me. I brought it back to my cell, wrapped it up carefully and posted it home, addressing it to mum. She told me in her next letter that she had framed it, so it would not fade away in some drawer. To this day, it is still hanging in her bedroom in her little bungalow. At the time, it was nice for me to feel that wee moment of family, even if it was in the middle of all that madness.

Listening to any form of racing on the radio, be it horses or the dogs, was a big pastime. The prisoners ran a betting syndicate, where you could bet two roll-ups on a horse. The Lincoln Hurdle was coming up. My brother Tom, who used to add a little piece onto the bottom of my mum's letters, wrote: *Pick a horse and I will back it for you.* So I opted for a horse called The Hartford, because I remembered it was also the name of a pub in Lisburn. It duly won, at twenty to one, a real outsider. Tom made many excuses why the money was never sent on! But he made up for it in more ways than one. He was very good to me and used to send me over great books to read. He would be working hard all week in the factory and on payday, before he hit the pub, he would go into a bookshop and buy me the latest bestsellers. He would buy the odd board game and put it into the box so that I had all the necessities to survive. As Tom was the eldest and lived at home with my parents, he was something like a second father to us all. He was always doing jobs for the others in the family and he never complained.

Doing time is a tricky business. You can't do it feeling sorry for yourself, for how you behaved or for what you did. If you try to do your time like that, the prisoners will wise up to you. If a man breaks down and starts crying once, most prisoners will look the other way. But the next time he does it they will start shouting at him.

It was an unwritten law that we were all in there, we

were all suffering, but we had to get on with it. If you were a weak link in the chain, some of the other prisoners would home in on you and give you a really hard time. You would be told to get lost, to get out of the wing, because they were not going to listen. Even though I heard through the grapevine that sometimes these prisoners picked on the others, I never saw any real brutality.

In ways, Brixton and Pentonville were easier than Ashfield. I had been done for robbery and the least I could be expected to do was two years. I had four months – my remand – done. That to me meant I only had another eight or ten months to go, because I would hopefully get a third off for remission. That was the way I was looking at it. So I focused on it.

Judgement day came. I was back before Knightsbridge Crown Court. I began to think that the two years were going to turn into twenty when I heard the first defence barrister. He was representing John Gayle. He had a stutter and he was so laborious that the judge was getting irritated with him. I thought: *We are going away big time.* Martin's barrister got up; he was a prosecutor who had decided to take on defence work. You wouldn't have noticed the difference. He was all but saying we deserved hard labour. I turned to my two mates in the dock and whispered, "We're crucified!" Then my barrister, Mr Greenfield, rose to his feet, and he started his speech, holding onto the pocket of his waistcoat. He said, "Your worship, not that I would wish to make light of this subject, but here we have our three desperadoes, Burke, Browne and Gayle. They decided to be robbers. Browne had his car damaged, Burke was the recipient of a cracked rib and Gayle received serious injuries from a beating. Now I wonder who came out the worst in all of this?" The judge actually smiled and suddenly it seemed that the whole case started to change.

It was going great for us. Kathy had even turned up for me. She got up in the witness box and cried, saying how much she wanted her husband back. She never mentioned that we were separated. The judge said he would remand the three of us in custody while he thought about it overnight. So the three of us went to Brixton for the night. I couldn't wait to show the boys the ropes! I felt like I was the business; they were asking me: "What do you do next? What do you do here?" I saw the sheer look of terror on Martin's face. It was as well he didn't get the four months on remand, because I don't think he could have hacked it. That's not bravado talking, because I could not have done it without the support of the people around me.

The next morning we were back in the court. The judge appeared in his red robes. Finally our case was called and we sat facing him in the dock. He said, "Well, I am going to put you out of your misery. You three are not going to prison." He gave us all a suspended two-year sentence. He fined me £150, as the Pakistani shopkeeper had said we took £300, so that went some way towards making amends. Greenfield told us afterwards that the judge had contacted a number of his contemporaries the previous night, canvassing opinion, because he was setting a precedent; judges did not hand down suspended sentences for robbery offences. Three of the other judges had suggested he let us off with suspended sentences. Greenfield talked the judge around on the day itself, and said that, although I had a record, it was for drug use, and none of us had ever seriously been robbers. He also pointed out that nobody had been physically hurt, apart from ourselves. Rightly or wrongly, they looked on me as the ring-leader, but I had already served four months in prison on remand and that was the equivalent of a six-month sentence. So we walked free at the end of May.

Chapter 20

I was never to forget people like Bill who had helped me to serve my remand. Bill and I formed a strong friendship. Indirectly, this friendship led me to my daughter Emma.

While we had been on remand, Bill and I had said that if we were to get out, by any miracle, then we would write to each other and let the other know. That kind of promise is rarely kept, but this one was. When I got out of Brixton, I was twenty-three, and I headed straight home to Lisburn. I decided to have a nice quiet life – again. One of the first things I did was to write to Bill. He was still on remand and I told him I had got a two-year suspended sentence. A short while later I got a letter from Bill, telling me that he too had got off with a suspended sentence. He had settled in Finchley in North London and was working behind the bar of a pub, and staying there in digs, as he had no home to return to. He had no access to his son and I don't know if this was out of choice or because of circumstances. It was a subject we never discussed. But Bill asked me if I would like to come over to London for a holiday.

In Lisburn, I had finally decided that my system was clear of drugs, but I was again deceiving myself, because I had replaced them with drink. I got a job in a local hospital as a porter and I worked hard for the next ten months, usually bumping into my old drinking cronies in the A&E. During that time I went over to visit Bill on three occasions. Typically, each time I went over I tried to convince myself that this was a chance to recreate the old lifestyle I yearned for – chasing the hippy dream, chasing after old friends who had got married and moved on, chasing after something that had happened years before but that would never have a chance of happening again. Ultimately I would find out that I had no power to recreate all the things I was trying to cling onto.

On one of these holidays, I met a girl called Trish. She had long blonde hair and she looked great! Trish worked as a secretary. It wasn't a whirlwind romance; when I met her for the first time, I didn't fall in love. I knew she was going out with another guy. The second time I went over, things were going badly between herself and her boyfriend Andy. I think she started to muck about with me to annoy him. We slept together. In my mind, I wanted to fall in love and wanted to turn it into a long-distance romance. So when I came back to Lisburn, I wrote to her and told her that I would like it if we could get together again.

Much to my shock and horror she wrote back, saying, "Well, that's great, I will come over." I didn't fancy this, so I went over instead to meet her parents, who were very middle-class people. I have no idea what they thought about us turning up on their doorstep, but Trish and I had nowhere to stay. After a few days with her parents, we headed to Kingston together and stayed in a bed-and-breakfast. While some of my old friends were there, the buzz had gone. The Three Fishes was still there so the odd time Trish and I would go over and get drunk. I had also begun to take drugs again – nothing heavy, just some dope at the weekends. But I was fooling myself that this was just some little social aside. Like every alcoholic knows, having a "social drink" is just madness and virtually impossible. It was the same way with my weekend drugs. But of course I was oblivious to what I was doing.

That was a crazy week or so. I was offered a job as a caretaker of a school in Kingston. The guy who interviewed me said that he would have accommodation thrown in but it would not be ready for another two months. This was all going pear-shaped! I thought, *This is not real; I can't live this life, being a caretaker, living with Trish.* We had even looked up Mrs Gari and stayed with her for a week or so. It was crazy, all serious stuff. I hadn't intended any of this to happen. I was scared, thinking I was going to settle down. Trish seemed to think we could make a go of it. She thought, *We'll both work, have a social drink and settle down in between all that.* I knew that was not what I wanted. I went along with it but, in my mind, I always believed it would only last a short time. I saw it as a break from my regular life. I thought, *There is nothing solid in this relationship.* It had initially been a holiday romance but it was turning into a nightmare.

I decided I had to get away, but I had no money and neither had Trish. We were living on the streets. So, we took a mad notion: get to Lisburn and all our problems would be solved! Or so we thought. So while we elaborated on our plan a little more, we went to Heathrow Airport and lived rough on what little money we had. The plan was to get enough for a plane ticket home to Lisburn. I was going to phone home to ask for some money to be sent over but Trish came up with a better idea. She said, "I'll go to my sister and get the money, for you at least, if not for both of us." She smiled and I watched her walk away out the automatic doors. I was thinking: *Both of us?* I spent three days in that airport, sleeping on the benches, picking up biscuit crumbs that people had left behind, getting by on bits and pieces. I was a bit of a lost soul. But fair play to Trish, she turned up trumps and came back with the money for my ticket back to Ireland. Her sister had coughed up.

I find it difficult to describe the relationship I had with Trish. We hardly knew each other, but we were both looking for something. We knew deep inside that it was not each other that we were looking for but we went ahead with it anyway, thinking: *Well, why not? What harm?* We had nothing else in our lives, so why not hang onto each other? I never for a moment thought it had anything to do with addiction – that we both were addicts in the sense that we lived off each other. Of course, why would I think that; after all, I wasn't an addict, was I?

When I got home to Lisburn I wrote to Trish and she wrote back saying that she was staying with her sister in

Notting Hill, but was eager to get out of there. I felt that it was my duty as a gentleman to get a place for us in Lisburn. So I took my mum on a trip up to Hillsborough Park one Sunday and as we walked together I told her about my undying love for this girl Trish. In a sense, looking back, I know that this was wishful thinking. I wasn't being deceptive, I wasn't lying – I had actually convinced myself that it was going to be something special.

Mum told me that Trish wouldn't be able to stay with us but she suggested that we could get a place together in town. She was sympathetic, and because she was sympathetic, I knew Tom would be sympathetic also. I went to see Tom and he said, "Well, maybe we can find a place." I said, "If we have to go to the Housing Executive then it could be a long wait." Tom suggested, "Let's just put the word out and see if anybody has a vacant property."

Sure enough, within a few days a cousin told us that there was a three-bedroom terraced house available in Manor Estate in the centre of the town. The woman who had been offered it had turned it down, but no one else had been allocated it. We asked her if she minded if we took it and she said she didn't.

One night, Tom took me up to have a look around the outside of the house. He turned to me and asked, "Do you want this house?"

"Yes, I do."

"How much do you really want it?"

"Well . . . I *really* want it."

"OK, just keep an eye out."

With that, Tom took out a claw hammer and a chisel

and with one swipe he hacked the lock off the door. He changed the lock and we went inside.

You would think with all my criminal activity that I wouldn't have been nervous about something like this, but I was, mainly because it was in my own home town, but also because of the atmosphere on the streets at the time – the paramilitaries ruled, and they could do what they liked. I was really frightened; this was my first time back in Northern Ireland for any length of time and I didn't know what was going on politically.

I asked Tom, "Are you sure we can do this?"

"Of course we can do it."

"Well, will you stay with me tonight, until we get settled?"

Tom told me that the Housing Executive would be around in the morning telling us to get out. And I said, "What do we say?" And he said, "Say 'no'."

We had a drink that night and we slept on a couple of sleeping bags on the floor. Next morning there came a knock at the door – the Housing Executive people. I recognised one of them, Brian, because I had gone to school with him. Brian said, "Jackie, you shouldn't be in there." Tom opened the top window – he wouldn't even open the front door to them – and, in the Queen's English, shouted down, "Take yourselves out of here – you have no chance. We are claiming squatters' rights."

And that was that; you could take a house that easily in Northern Ireland in those days. They had only really started to bring people to court. So I told Trish to get on the next plane.

She came to my parents' house and met them and my

brothers. The meeting was very quick; everybody exchanged pleasantries over a cup of tea, and the brothers enquired about Trish's life, the usual civil questions. I got the feeling Raymond and Tom were hoping the relationship would work out for me. I think they wanted to see me put down some roots. So Trish and I settled in to Manor Estate in the summer of 1979.

Chapter 21

Now that Trish was over with me I began to think about
going back on drugs. I started taking speed and
barbiturates again. She took drugs but it was purely from
my bad influence – I had to do all the convincing. She
took a bit of speed, but Trish would rather have had a
nice glass of white wine. I really didn't think I was doing
her any harm. To me Trish was just a part-time user. When
I look back now, I can see my actions were immature. I
certainly wasn't acting like someone who was serious
about having a real relationship. Now I thank God that
Trish never became addicted, as she might well have
done, if I had pushed things a bit.

Living the squatter's life in the house, we were having
parties, everyone was smoking dope. It was just like the
old days. I met a guy called Alan who started to call to
the house for drink and drugs. He was to be a big
influence in my drug-taking life later on.

I was twenty-six and I was back on the medical prescriptions from the doctor and I got Trish prescriptions for drugs too; I told the doctor she needed them. So I was able to get double amounts and I was also selling some of it. It all went very well – all party, party, party – for about nine months. Then one day Trish told me she was pregnant and that her mum was coming over to visit.

Trish's mum arrived over. She went to visit my mum and dad with a pot plant as a gift. That summed up the clash of cultures. My dad didn't know what to do. My mum looked at the gift, dumbfounded, and muttered, "Thank you very much." Trish's mum then arrived at our house, took one look around and said, "My goodness, you haven't got a dishwasher!" There were only two of us. I didn't eat that much, because I was taking speed. I couldn't figure out why I needed a dishwasher.

Trish's mum stayed with us for almost a week in the squat. Before she went, she tried to kit the house out in the very latest mod cons. Trish's dad had a very senior job in the electricity service in the UK. One day Trish's mum said to her, "Come on. Let's go down the town." They went into the Lisburn electrical shop and she pointed to loads of appliances and said they would take them. Money was no object – brand new cooker, dishwasher, washing machine, all of that. Of course, she wanted them at discount prices, so she flashed her card, as if it had taken her into Buckingham Palace and back again. But she couldn't use it in Northern Ireland, so she had the indignity of having to write out a cheque for the full amount. I had a good laugh at the situation but Trish and I had a big row, the first of many, over the whole thing.

Trish was not sure how our future was looking. She decided that she wanted to have the baby back in England, so she got on a plane a week or so after her mother. So there I was in a half-empty house, with all these brand new shiny electrical appliances around me. Eventually I decided to go over to Trish to try to work it out but it failed. I knew my relationship with Trish would not have worked, even if I had been as sober as a judge.

Even so, I knew I was facing fatherhood again, and this time, I knew the baby was mine. I had been there by Trish's side throughout all the hospital appointments and I had been looking forward to the birth. But I knew I was not in any good shape as a prospective parent. I would have to clean up my act – again. So I went back to Northern Ireland and signed myself into Antrim Hospital, the same place I had attended in 1973. I decided to make another big effort to get off drugs, but this itself was becoming a routine way of life for me. In a way, going into rehab was an addiction in itself, but I never knew it. I only stayed there for a few weeks. It was almost comical – I would ring Trish from rehab and she would ring me from the maternity ward in the hospital in England.

When Trish had had her twelve-week scan, while we were living as squatters, we had been told that there might be a possibility of twins, but it was never confirmed. When the time came in 1981, Trish went to a hospital near her mum's to give birth. I was in still in rehab back in the North. After Emma was born, Trish screamed that there was another baby in there. But the doctors insisted that there wasn't, and so little Jenny died in the womb.

I wasn't there for Trish, for Emma's birth or for little Jenny. Trish contacted me and told me the full story. I took the call in one of the public phone booths in the rehab. I listened, staring at the dirt-encrusted dial in front of me, as Trish told me I had a daughter and I had lost another. Between checking out of rehab and getting the flight sorted, it took me the best part of a week to actually get over to London to be at Trish's bedside. But once I took Emma into my arms – a little crying bundle in a pink blanket – I broke down with emotion. She was so beautiful.

I hadn't thought much about what I was going to do, or how I would react as a new father, but when I was standing there, holding Emma in my arms, it was as if the whole bad world had drifted away, and her face was the only real light shining in it. My little Jenny had already been laid to rest. I missed my own daughter's funeral. So I began to think: What sort of a father was I? I felt a loss that was unexplainable – I had known Jenny, yet I had never met her in this life. Trish, naturally, was very upset about Jenny and I cried along with her.

Then I began to get angry and the more I thought about her death, the angrier I got with the world. I stormed into a doctor's office and ranted that something should have been done to save my daughter. I wanted to know how the hospital could have made a mistake when we had previously been told that there was a possibility of twins. Trish was inconsolable over it. The doctor said that to find out the actual cause of death would be a long drawn-out process, and while he understood that I wanted to go ahead with it, and make someone responsible, Trish was not up to it.

After Emma was born, Trish and I got back together. I was now a father, if initially in name only, for the second time. I intended to do my best to make things work for Emma's sake. I loved her dearly, but I was still a very insecure drug addict, although I didn't realise this at the time. I was uncertain about my relationship with Trish. I felt we had no similar outlook on life. If anything, she had become more settled than before. Motherhood had matured her, while I felt I was just looking in at my life as it unfolded.

However, I felt protective towards Trish and we formed a close bond of friendship. Her mum was not pleased. Trish and I decided between us that she would come out of hospital with the baby and that I would go back to sort things out in Lisburn before I came back to join them. She rented a bungalow in Caterham-on-the-Hill, south of London, very up-market. She sent for me and I came over. The first Sunday I was there her mum arrived with the Sunday papers for Trish, as she usually did. I opened the front door and when she saw me, she slammed the papers into my hand and said, "Tell my daughter I won't be back." And she kept her word; she didn't come near us until about nine months later, after I got a job. Then she was one of the first to visit us – I was now, apparently, "acceptable".

Before this, though, I was dipping into a little speed and I was also drinking. Any "right-minded" people might ask: *How could he do that?* I was father to a newborn child; what kind of a monster was I? Didn't I love my child? I did love Emma, but the point was that the whole cycle of drink led to breaking into a doctor's surgery which led to getting into trouble with the police.

Whenever I got drunk, the first thing I wanted to do was to get some "real" drugs. So the cycle began. But that cycle had not been broken and it would not get broken until many years later, when I became a follower of Christ. I was totally in love with drugs, more than my daughter, more than my partner, more than God, more than life itself.

Trish and I broke up yet again, but I decided to get my act together and find a job. I had a second chance to be a father and I was going to take it. I did not want just to visit Emma; I wanted to try again to be a real dad. It was all or nothing this time. Again, in my own head I wasn't an addict, so I could conquer drugs.

I had quite fancied driving a bread van around London, so when a job came up, delivering bread, I went for it. Even on the day of the interview I took a bit of speed. The chap interviewing hadn't a clue and said to one of the drivers, "You go with him and see if he can handle it." I drove him around Croydon, taking a corner on two wheels but amazingly he said, "OK, Paddy, you've got the job." I couldn't lose a job even if I tried! But once I got the job, the speed was put aside.

Now there was a problem. I had to start at five o'clock in the morning. The headquarters was in Croydon, while we were in Caterham. I had no transport. Trish's brother had a bicycle and I borrowed it. Here is how my day would go: I would get up at three o'clock in the morning, feed the baby and put her back into her cot when I was sure she was content and sleeping. I would kiss Trish goodbye, get on my bike and cycle about five miles to the bakery, in all weathers. Then I would work all morning and come back at three in the afternoon, have an hour's sleep and then get up, feed the baby, make the tea, wash the dishes, feed the baby and go to bed.

This was the same guy who, just a month before, had broken into a doctor's surgery to steal prescriptions. That was the contrast. That was what I could do when I put my mind to it. I really got into it. That period marked a fresh start. And then one morning, a few weeks into the job, I was late, and the rule was very strict about being on time, so I lost the job.

However, I didn't resort back to drink and drugs. I started looking for another job. But then we realised that, because we were living in rented accommodation with a child, we could get our rent paid from the dole, and that was our biggest outlay. So, for a while, it didn't make sense to work. We settled down for a few weeks with me on the dole. Trish was doing a little bit of part-time cleaning. She enjoyed that – she didn't have to do it, but she liked being out of the house for a couple of hours – and I just enjoyed being a father to Emma. I was falling in love with my daughter more and more each day, because we spent a lot of time together. Trish was a great mother, but during this period, I looked after Emma more than she did, because I was at home more often. I used to take her for walks in the pram, enjoyed my time with her and did all the things a good father should do. I really wanted to be a father and to do it right.

Of course, I made a couple of blunders. I went out and got drunk a couple of times. Signs of the past lifestyle would rear their head, but nothing really could have split us up. I hardly took any drugs at all during that period and my drinking was moderate, at least compared to what I had been doing previously. Looking back, it was a sort of denial. At the time I didn't see the wrong I was doing. I thought: *It's unreasonable for anyone to expect me to stay off drugs as well as stay sober.* On reflection, I was treading water and would never change.

Chapter 22

I decided to look for another job. I had this idea that I would be a better father if I could provide for my family, but also I was getting bored being a "house husband". One day I walked down to the job centre to see if there was anything going. The unemployment office in Caterham was about the size of a small living room – people were just not unemployed, so nobody went there. But one of the first cards I saw on the board read: *"Gardener required, driving involved, apply within."* I took the card over to the woman sitting behind the desk, her grey hair up in a bun. I said, "I'd like to apply for this job."

She looked at me and said, "Are you sure?"

"Yes, I am very sure."

"But this is for Lady MacNeile Dixon of Lagham Manor."

"So?"

"Can you drive?"

"Of course, yes."

"Do you know gardening?"

"Yes," I said, and added, "are we doing the interview now or should I see the woman herself?"

"Very well – hold on."

She lifted the phone and rang Lady Dixon. She said, "I've got a chap here who is interested in your job, shall I send him along?" In other words, probably not. She obviously did not know Lady Dixon, who turned out to be a fantastic woman.

An arrangement was made for an interview. I put on a three-piece suit, shirt and tie. Trish's mum looked after Emma, as Trish had to come too – Lady Dixon was also looking for somebody to keep the kitchen. The best thing was, accommodation would be provided as part of the job.

It was a sunny day as we strolled through the entrance into Lagham Manor. We walked up this long, potholed driveway, which was probably kept that way to deter burglars and trespassers. It was hot and we had to walk a half-mile. I kept saying, "This could be really good." At the same time I was thinking: *What am I going to say? What do I know about gardening?*

As we turned the bend the road suddenly opened out and there in front of us was a beautiful country manor house. We were taken aback. It had picturesque flowers and shrubs growing up against the walls. It was so quaint-looking; it looked like an oil painting. I went up and rapped on the front door. Nobody answered, so I rapped again, and this time an old lady came around the corner. She was in a navy boiler suit, wearing a big floppy sun hat and she had grey hair curling around her face. She was probably about eighty years of age, yet she came bouncing over.

"Are you Jack?"

"Yeah, I'm Jack."

"OK Jack; let's have a look at the place."

I started walking around with this woman and all the time she was continually talking: "This tree needs to be cut back . . . planting here . . . and what do you know about gardening?"

I answered, "Not a lot, I may as well be honest with you."

"Ah well! You're Irish – you'll know how to grow spuds!"

So we walked on and chatted. When we got to the end of the walk, she told me, "If you want the job, Jack, you can have it."

"Great, that's brilliant! I will be a quick learner."

She was pleased to have Trish there – her job would be a matter of keeping the Manor House tidy and clean. That began our stay in Lagham Manor.

During that interview I didn't tell Lady Dixon we had a child as well. So the next day I phoned her and said, "There's something I should have told you about – we have a wee baby." Lady Dixon took a deep breath. "That's OK," she said. She was just a wonderful woman, one of the nicest women you could ever meet. She showed us our accommodation, which was like a chocolate-box painting of a little cottage, with beautiful gardens for Emma to play in. It was all going to be so perfect.

As well as gardener, I became Lady Dixon's chauffeur.

One day I was taking her on a trip to see her sister and I started talking to her about her life. She told me about the first time she was on a plane, on a trip to Paris. In her matter-of-fact way she told me, "I was in a Second World War bomber that had been refitted for normal travel."

"Were you not frightened?"

"No, not a bit!"

"What was the plane like inside?"

"Oh, we got into the plane," she recalled, "and there was a wicker chair bolted to the ground – no seat belt, nothing. The plane took off. I was quite enjoying the flight but not so much the jigging. Then the door of the cockpit – if you could call it a cockpit – the door flew open as we hit a bit of turbulence, and I saw this chap sitting on an orange box crate, he was like a mechanic in overalls and he had some sort of tool like a spanner in his hand. I thought to myself, 'Oh my God, is this the chap we are depending on?' But it was exciting, especially as that was my first trip to France in a plane." She had been there as a young girl and she reminisced about every detail. She had become fascinated by a certain kind of green bean that was growing in a particular field. So she had wandered into the field and cut a couple of slips, brought them back to England and grew them in the manor.

Lady Dixon had a remarkable amount of knowledge. She talked about the history of Lagham Manor in a very direct way; there was never any snobbishness in the woman. She said, "Don't call me Lady Dixon, call me Lal or Mrs, but don't call me lady." She told me stories about the Manor being taken over by the troops during the war, how it was used as a place to help the sick and the injured and how she ran errands for the British and American troops. She was a fantastic lady and everything about the Manor held a memory for her. One day I was walking into the place where she stored the apples and she told me that the seeds for the apples were over two hundred years old. I loved the sense of history about the place.

For her birthday, Lady Dixon's daughter decided to throw her a big party, but she was really quite uncomfortable about the whole thing. Typical of her, she invited Trish and me to the party and asked us to bring little Emma. I thought I'd better put a decent shirt on and dress myself up a bit for it! The party was like something out of a fairytale. The whole of the lawn had been decked out and prepared with little tables with linen cloths on them. People started arriving in their twos and threes. One guy, an old buffer of a colonel with the walrus moustache, came up the driveway with a golden-handled stick. He walked over to me and whispered conspiratorially: "Jack, which side are you on?" I said: "Well, actually, I am the gardener." He looked disappointed. Then the young grandnephew appeared in a Morgan sports car with his scarf flying. That was the type of people we were rubbing shoulders with. Lady Dixon treated us as complete equals. You could understand, when you saw how different her relatives were to her, why she didn't like changes. She had a great deal of humility.

We spent about a year in Lagham Manor. Lady Dixon liked the fact that I was Irish. I would just say things as I saw them, I worked hard and she didn't have to ask me for anything twice. She was someone that I responded to in those days, because she had a right to ask so much and asked so little. Because of that, I gave her twice as much. The work was fascinating; for example, there was an orchard producing beautiful apples, but nobody could get near them because the orchard was all overgrown. Lady Dixon said to me, "There is no way of getting all that cut down, except through the use of a scythe." I'd never lifted a scythe in my life, but I certainly learned how to use it that day. She had one of the old wooden-handled ones, so I started in that field and I went at it from morning until evening and I flattened it. I would not have done that for anybody but her.

It was a beautiful place for Emma to grow up in. She was five months old when we first went to live there. It was the right environment for me, for all of us. Imagine waking up in the morning and you are already at your workplace; you look out your lovely cottage window and there is your garden, your orchard, your wood-cutting shed, your trees and plants, and you get to go out into that idyllic place to work for the whole day. I had a job with a good wage and I had a car to drive. I had everything. I was one hundred per cent behind it. I was very pleased and very proud of what I was achieving. For the first time in my life, I had a purpose.

But things were not going so well between Trish and myself. We started arguing again. I felt that Trish was getting more controlling. All the time at Lagham Manor, I didn't take drugs, but I did drink. I was drinking at the weekends, but it began to get worse when Trish's mother started to visit us more. It seemed that the more I gave, the less I got. I know that sounds like a cliché but I was working hard all week and I would have a cigarette and a couple of beers at the weekend, but it wasn't good enough for Trish. The Irish in me, the rebel in me, would explode every now and again and I would head to the off-licence down the street and drink myself stupid. I just didn't think it was fair, that I was working hard, and yet this was never enough.

Of course, in hindsight, I can see that this might have been a result of addictive behaviour – that saying "it just isn't fair" was an excuse for me to drink. Now I see clearly that all that was asked of me was to be moderate in all things, which was reasonable. However, at the time, this seemed totally unreasonable. Yet even today, looking back, I can see that while this had been a period of opportunity to build a lasting relationship, it could never have worked, with or without the drink and drugs. Trish and I were two completely different people, with little or nothing in common, except Emma.

The arguments between myself and Trish were not always drink-fuelled. We would have arguments about lots of different things. One time I decided to invite my parents over. This was the first time in my life that I wanted to show off in front of them. I had finally got something that I had achieved and that I was proud of. Two weeks before they arrived, Trish decided she was not going to speak to me anymore. I could never stand that. If you hate me, I want you to shout at me – don't give me the silent treatment. It is so unemotional, it's so unreal.

The day before my parents arrived she acted as a normal partner. My parents arrived and we gave them a tour of Lagham Manor. Dad and mum were a little overwhelmed, and when they met with Lady Dixon they didn't know what to say! "Call me Lal," she said to mum. "Yes, Lady Dixon", said mum. I was so proud showing my parents around this beautiful place. They thought that, at last, I had made good. They hoped, now that I had a family of my own, that this was the beginning of the end of my drug lifestyle.

Trish and I did the tourist thing. We got Emma all dressed up and brought the whole family to London. We went down the Thames on a boat and visited Buckingham Palace. All the while Trish was the perfect hostess and got on quite well with my mum and dad.

But as soon as they had gone it was back to the silent treatment again. Whenever I saw that, it snapped something in me that said this was not love, this was not respect and I was not going to put up with it. I know, looking back, that I was difficult to live with. Trish was a new mother, trying to keep our family together while battling with her own mother about how she hadn't picked a "bad one". Trish was probably on eggshells waiting for the next drunken episode and realising more and more that I was not someone who could have a "social" drink and leave it at that.

After a third week of this, it all blew up and we had a huge row. I shouted at her, "If you go down that driveway without speaking to me, I guarantee, I will not be here when you get back." She walked off as if I hadn't spoken and I will never forget it. Emma was sitting in the wee pushchair and Trish pushed her a few feet down the driveway. Emma looked back at me and waved her little hand to say *bye bye*.

That was the last time I saw my daughter Emma.

Chapter 23

I went back into the house, packed my suitcase, and raided the wine cellar in the manor. I thought: *I'm gonna have a drink before I leave.* But of course I got drunk and fell asleep. I woke up to Trish standing over me, ranting and raving. In a drunken delirium I took a TV set and threw it out the window. It was sheer madness; I was out of my mind on drink. She phoned for the police and when they arrived she kept shouting: "He's on drugs! He's on drugs!" But I wasn't. I had a fight with the police and hurt a couple of them as they bundled me into the police car. But because she had been shouting about drugs, the police were worried about taking me to the police station, so decided they would take me to a hospital to be checked over.

I woke up the next morning in what I thought was a police cell. Sitting at the end of the room was a young man; I assumed him to be a CID police officer. I asked him what I had been arrested for. He asked me, "Where do you think you are?"

"I'm in a police cell."

"No, you're not. You are in Nethern Hospital and this is St John's Ward – it's a lock-up ward. You have been sectioned."

I'd never known what "being sectioned" meant until I found out later that morning, when after a young nurse helped me get washed and dressed, I was brought in to meet the doctor, who sat like a Buddha behind his desk. I sat and poured out my heart to him, saying, "This is all a misunderstanding. I have a job to go back to, and a girlfriend and a baby. Can I just get out of here?" He said, "Mr Burke, you will not be leaving here until I decide so. You have assaulted two police officers and you are being put under Section 48." I would be there for as long as he wanted me to be, whether that was a day or the rest of my life. The sheer fear of that is indescribable – to know that your freedom lies in one man's hands, a man who doesn't even know you. In prison, at least I knew when I would get out. This was different.

I began to sober up. I thought: *I could turn this to my advantage; if they think I am on drugs, I could play the helpless addict.* I was angling to get out of the police charging me. So when a young doctor arrived I told him I was on barbiturates, amphetamines and a whole mixture of drugs. He gave me an injection and I conked out.

When I woke up, I found that my suitcase, with all my clothes, had been brought into the hospital. I discovered that Lady Dixon had brought it in and the only reason that she didn't stay and ask to speak with me was that, in her own words, "It would have proved too much for me". She wrote to my mother and father, a letter my mother would show me later on, saying that she didn't want to take sides in the argument between Trish and me, but she felt that what had happened was sad. She wanted my mother to know that she valued my friendship and all the work I had done.

I really felt the loss of that wonderful environment, the loss of my relationship and of my daughter. I knew that, if things had been different, I could have happily lived my life there.

I was locked up with some very sad cases, some of them very terrifying. One guy, Stan, was almost like a neo-Nazi who terrorised all the other patients. Being Irish I found it hard to bend under his tyranny! We would have some showdowns during the weeks that followed. He used to march up and down the ward staring madly at people. If you dared to meet his gaze he would start a fight. He had already tried to strangle another patient with one of the toilet chains. It was a matter of survival in my mind because I was with people who were psychologically damaged while, for all my drug-taking, I still had my brain. So I was constantly thinking: *How do I get out of here?*

Everything was contained in my ward, including washing facilities. There was a cell-type door at the end of it and an ordinary door, both of which had to be opened by someone else if I needed to get out. At least I could walk around in my own clothes. As well as the more extreme cases like Stan, there were gentler, more ordinary people. One man, Phil, was in his fifties, and every day he read the Bible. So even there, God's little touches were all around me, but I never felt them. Or rather I chose not to feel them. But even though I had lost faith over the years, something was still pulling me towards Him.

There was a wee guy called Sam who was severely disabled and had no ability to do anything for himself. He could only take liquid food. He died while I was in the ward. I was amazed at the dedication of the nurses because he wasn't a pretty sight. He was dirty and when he died some of the liquid food came out of his mouth and the staff gave him the kiss of life. I remember watching it, horrified.

Thank God for the nurse who was the first one to talk to me while I was in there, the guy who was there for me when I woke up. Paul kept me sane and emphasised that all I had to do was just hold on, that it was a matter of convincing the psychiatrists that I was normal. He knew that would happen eventually; he knew I didn't belong there, but I had to wait. The psychiatrist had a point to prove. Three weeks later, I was released after my probation officer visited and told me Trish did not want me back. He said there was a possibility that he could get me into a probation hostel in Aldershot.

To get residency I had to face a surreal entrance interview from those already living there. I was brought out of the psychiatric ward for the interview. I was given a tough grilling by the residents. They asked questions like: "How do we know you will never take drugs again?" They really gave me a hard time but once I was accepted and moved into the probation hostel the first thing the residents asked me, ironically, was, "Can you get us some drugs?"

I stayed in Aldershot for a while. But I knew after a few weeks that there was going to be no possibility of surviving in England on my wits. I thought I would only end up in the Nethern Hospital or Probation Hospital again, or worse. I had to go home. So I phoned my parents. They weren't exactly happy at the idea of me coming home again, because by now they had had enough too. But they loved me, and reluctantly agreed that I could come home. I know they felt that I was a drug addict, but at least I would be better off living close to them than out of sight.

Even after I moved back to Lisburn, I never gave up on Emma. It was the first time in my whole selfish life that I ever experienced real grief. For the first time I really knew what it was to miss someone more than myself. I would phone Trish up, especially when I had a few drinks on me, and ask to speak to Emma. Trish, to her credit, allowed me to make those phone calls in the beginning. I made loads of noise at the time – that I was going to go over there and take Emma and claim my rights to her. But then I had a think about it: I was a junkie (but still didn't admit it), Northern Ireland was still reeling from the Hunger Strikes, violence was everywhere – and I wanted to bring my daughter over to all that? I didn't think any judge would have given me a chance for custody.

It took about three or four years before I finally stopped trying. I talked to everybody about Emma – the people around me, other addicts, my family. But I became a bore after a while, because every time I went out in their company, I ended up weeping in the corner. I would go home and sit in my room, staring at a photo taken on a warm summer's evening in front of Lagham Manor. I was holding Emma in my arms, looking lovingly down at this little blonde-haired bundle, while my mum put her arm around me and smiled proudly into the camera.

Chapter 24

For the next couple of years I stayed at home, living with mum and dad. I continued to take my prescription drugs and did odd jobs here and there. The pull of London was still very strong, though, and I often felt like jacking everything in and heading back over there. Of course, the good old days were now long gone. I had nobody to go back to. All the people I knew from my hippy days were well and truly scattered; some had died, some had settled down into a regular nine-to-five life. Most of them had got caught in the net; it seemed like it was only people like me who had slipped through. In Lisburn, the odd jobs didn't last long. I tried my hand again as a porter in the hospital and I also worked in a factory. But I could never settle myself.

Throughout the early 1980s, I made my best efforts to come off drugs, as much for my parents' sake as my own. I fell back on the rehab system and signed myself into a couple of places. I was determined that I would get clean. All the time, though, I had it in my own head: *At least I am still decent. I am not and will never become a junkie.* As I showed on many occasions, getting off the drugs wasn't the problem; it was staying off them.

One of those rehabs was run by an ex-priest. I went in on the "suggestion" of my probation officer, and I got a real sense that, there, I might be able to make it work. This place was recognised as one of the best. It had therapy groups where everyone would sit around and talk about their life. I thought they were all mad!

But as usual, I screwed it up. I met a girl while I was in there, and we went out for a drink together the second week. Of course, this was against the rules. However, she was allowed to stay while I was thrown out.

My brother Tom had always tried to help me to keep off drugs. When I was living back at home he would take me out for walks, listen to me and give me some advice. He had lived in the family home all his life and had never married. He was the mainstay of the family as my parents got on in years.

It was 1986 and Tom was thirty-eight years old. I was still on the prescription drugs. We decided to go for a holiday together on the coast and stayed there in a rented caravan. We were having a great time, the drink was flowing, and I was happy because I was on the waiting list for a new flat. I had finally realised that I needed to move out of home; it was getting a little bit claustrophobic. I broke off from the holiday early, because I was contacted and told I had been given a flat. I was in heaven and I couldn't wait to see it. It turned out to be a nice little council flat. I decided that this was it – I was going to make a good go of things once and for all. I began to take a pride in the place, decorating it and kitting it out with little bits of furniture I got, some from mum and other pieces I came across in town.

I badgered Tom about coming over and laying down some carpet for me. Tom was a great carpenter and was always doing odd jobs. But he kept putting off this particular job, until eventually I wore him down about it and he said he would be over. It was a particularly warm day. Tom got stuck into the job. After a while, I noticed he was not looking too good. He was pale and sweating. "Are you all right?" I asked. He looked up at me and said, "Can I lie down for a bit in the spare room?" I said, "Yes, of course." I poured him a drink. After he had the drink and on his way to bed, he looked back at me and said, "I'll try to sleep this off, but if mum and dad come over here, tell them I'll be staying the night – and don't bother waking me."

I went to the downstairs flat to a party with my new neighbour Gerry. Later that evening my parents arrived to see if Tom wanted to come home with them. I said: "I'll go and check, but he said he wanted to stay." I went into the room; he didn't respond to me calling him so I gently shook him and his head moved and air came out of his mouth. I just thought he was breathing, but in hindsight, I don't know whether or not he had already died. I went back downstairs and told mum and dad that Tom was sound asleep. I said, "Sure, he can stay with me." They said, "OK," and drove off.

I went back to the party and returned to my own flat

early the next morning, where I fell asleep on the sofa. Later that morning I woke up, made a cup of tea and went into my brother. He was not moving and when I put my hand on his arm, I felt a cold sensation go right through me. I realised that he was dead. I went into a state of shock. I ran downstairs and asked one of my neighbours to come up, just to confirm it. I thought I was in a nightmare. Gerry checked Tom's pulse. He turned to me and said, "Yes, your brother is dead."

I was distraught. "What will I do now?"

"You will have to call an ambulance and the police."

I went around to see my other brother Raymond. When I told him about Tom, he thought I was out of my head on drugs. He got me into his car and drove at high speed back to my new flat. He almost parked the car up on the kerb, nearly taking the front wheels off. He was very upset. He was convinced I was making the whole thing up, or that I was in a drugged state. Raymond walked into the little room in the flat, took one look at Tom and began to cry. This was a reality check for me. I now knew that Tom had left us.

What happened next was blurred because I began to weep uncontrollably, but I know Raymond phoned for an ambulance and for the police. Of course when they arrived the police knew me, so although they were sympathetic when they saw me, they were also fishing for information. They asked me if anything had happened during the night and questioned me to find out if I had been in any way responsible for my brother's death. I told them about the drink I had poured for him. But it seemed obvious to most of us, just by looking at Tom, that he had had a heart attack. We thought his death was natural, if you could call it that.

Looking back, I often wonder whether Tom had known that there was something seriously wrong with him. Did he want to save my parents the devastation of finding him dead?

Even in the moments after discovering Tom dead, there was still the drug addict lurking inside me, wanting to be given attention. I stood beside the doctor as she confirmed his death, along with the time and place. As she was leaving I asked her to give me some Valium. She said, "Why do you want that?" I said, "My parents – they will need it." She said, "If your parents need that then let them contact me themselves. I am not giving you anything." I then saw Tom being put into a black body bag and he was taken off to the hospital mortuary.

Now we had to tell our parents. Raymond and I went around to the house in total silence in the car. As we came through the front door, my mother and father both got up off the sofa. They saw our faces. My brother said, straight out, "Tom's dead." My father doubled over as though someone had kicked him in the stomach. My mother couldn't stand and she sat down and began to weep quietly. I don't know how long we all sat like that but it seemed like a very long time.

Now, like most people dealing with such a trauma, your mind goes into a different place where it deals with the practical. Family members and friends had to be told. So Raymond and I went around to see our cousins and our aunts, and informed them all of the tragic news. Of course for every member of the family that we met that

day, it was the same result. They met us with a smile at
the door and we left them in tears. Tom had gone and no
one would ever take his place. He had helped everyone in
our extended family down through the years in one way
or another – decorating homes for aunts, sharing happy
times on holidays with cousins. I just can't overstate it:
the heart of our family was ripped out.

Over the next few days the police called. There was
going to be a post mortem because of the circumstances
in which Tom had died. When we found out that he had
died of alcohol poisoning, I was relieved, in my own
selfish way. During those first few days since his death I
had played over and over in my mind the events of that
night. *Had* something happened? I wondered if the drugs
had made me do something that I had just shut out of my
mind afterwards. Was I his killer? Once we knew the
cause of death, I knew that I had not killed him, even
though I had poured that one drink for him. But later I
was to feel differently.

Chapter 25

With Raymond's help I was able to look after the practical arrangements for Tom's funeral. I kept going – partly on sheer strong will, partly on speed, but mainly because I had this determination that things would be done right.

There must have been a thousand people at Tom's funeral. He was a most popular man. Standing at the graveside, watching him being lowered into the grave, I realised that people were still coming into the cemetery. There were Catholics and Protestants, Republicans and Loyalists. One of the characters in the crowd was the head of the UDA; another was a Catholic Alliance Party member. Both arrived and had to look at each other over the coffin. I like to think Tom had a laugh at that.

We were a tight family and I thank God that we three brothers were all on good speaking terms when Tom passed away. When Tom died, our supports were pulled away and each member of the family went off into their own little shells. My other brother, Raymond, was married and he had his wife to turn to. But my mother and father never really talked about Tom's death. I left the flat and came back home to live with them.

A few weeks after the funeral we planned a little trip together. So mum, dad and I went for a short holiday in Newcastle, County Down. Every day I watched my mum get up and go out for a walk along the promenade while my dad just sat inside in the hotel, looking out the window, watching her. Normally they would have been at each other's side all the time, but not this time. I was still taking drugs and they didn't know about it – speed and barbiturates, the usual cocktail. I began to realise that the funeral was over, the break was half over, and it would be time for me to start dealing with my pain.

In the immediate weeks and months after Tom had died, I began to realise that I needed to make some tough decisions. I knew myself well enough to know that I was going to be going on a real bender – the bender to end all benders. So I began to organise getting more drugs. But I also did something that I don't regret doing. I went to see my perennial probation officer, and told him what had happened. I couldn't face going back to my flat, to the place where Tom had died, and I needed to get out of my parents' house where I was staying. I told him, "Look, I don't know how you need to do this, but I have to get into a hostel."

"But you're living at home with your parents."

"I don't want to anymore. I know what's lying ahead and I need to be away from them, out of their sight."

I was planning my own death. But my death would not be unexpected or instant like Tom's. Mine was going to be a slow decline. I wanted to increase my consumption of prescription drugs and alcohol. I wanted out; I wanted to end my life. I was planning to go out with a bang.

So I got the probation officer to fix me up in the Simon Community hostel in Belfast and I lived there for about eight months. It was a typical hostel, full of winos, drug addicts, dossers of all description – all seeking a roof, all seeking a higher high. We used to share bottles of wine and drugs together. I would wander around the streets, tapping people for money. Drink was at the centre of everything. I would also have prescription drugs given to me, but mainly we were on the tap for alcohol. It was just an endless round of taking drugs, drinking and sleeping, eating the odd meal in the hostel and getting back out onto the street again.

My parents drove down to Belfast every Sunday in their little Mini car. They knew I would be sober on Sunday for some reason. They would park in the railway car park at Central Station. They would sit in their wee car waiting for me. Some days I wouldn't show up. But when I did arrive, I would open the passenger door and get into the back seat. I would talk about how well things were going for me. Of course, I was lying my head off. "That's great, son," they would reply. They knew rightly it was probably all lies.

Mum and dad would look into the back seat at me, their youngest son, sitting almost comically stuffed into this tiny car. They would look at my hair, my face, my eyes, my large duffle coat and the shoes I was wearing. They would take it all in. Whatever they felt at those moments in their heart, I didn't want to know; I didn't care. All I wanted was the money for my drugs.

Then there would be a lull in the conversation as my father passed me back a couple of hundred cigarettes and twenty-five pounds. I'm sure he knew it wasn't going on anything sensible. They kept this up for months after Tom's death. I'm sure it was one of the last places they ever wanted to be.

In the next year I did my best to achieve my goal. I drank more than I had ever drunk before in my life. It was almost like a subconscious desire. There I was, trying to drown out the empty feelings again. Even though it had been proved otherwise, I became convinced that Tom's death was my fault. It never occurred to me that nobody could die of just one large drink. No, I had done it – I had given Tom that drink and I had taken the rap. I felt I had destroyed my whole family.

A few times my parents had come across me in floods of tears over it all, and they tried to reassure me that it was not my fault. Tom's death had probably been due to the drinking he had been doing on holiday, and that had probably built up the level of alcohol poisoning in his body. But still no one could convince me that I wasn't responsible.

The day of Tom's funeral my father had leaned over the open coffin, kissed him on the forehead and said, "Don't worry, son, you have just gone a little bit before me, I'll not be long behind." He was to keep to his word: within nineteen days of the first anniversary of Tom's death, my father died of a heart attack. I would say it was more of a broken heart. Dad had never lifted his head from the day Tom died.

Chapter 26

It was a year and a half after Tom's death and dad had passed away a few months before. I was still living a life of hard drinking. I had got out of the hostel and was in another flat now in Lisburn, by myself. I wanted to spend more and more time alone; that was the pattern to my life. One day, in 1987, I was drinking a lot and I went down to the health centre and stole some prescription pads. I had money from the dole and I got a taxi to Newcastle. I managed to pass a couple of forged prescriptions there. I sauntered down to the beach and joined up with the "Beach Boys" – a gang of winos who lived rough among the sand dunes. I spent a couple of days with them, drinking and sleeping in the rough grass and on the sheltered parts of the beach. I was careful, though, with the prescriptions, I had hidden them in a hedge up at the other end of town.

I hooked up with a guy called Jimmy. I got wee Jimmy to pass a prescription for me in Castlewellan near

Newcastle. It was for some barbiturates and I immediately took them. I wrote out another prescription, but with the barbiturates in me I could hardly write. My handwriting was very shaky and messed up, with the word *mitte* written all over the place. I took it into the centre of Newcastle and tried to pass it. I was duly arrested.

I was brought down to the station. I had two extra prescriptions hidden on me. The policeman asked if he needed to strip-search me; I am sure I was a sight, having been sleeping rough. To his relief I said, "No" – and he didn't. He decided to charge me with prescription forgery and he released me on police bail. Outside, what I should have done was got the bus and gone home. Instead I wrote out another prescription and tried to pass it in another pharmacy. So within an hour I was back in the police station again with another charge, this time for all the prescriptions, because they found the others on me, and there would be no bail for me.

I was kept overnight in the cell and the following day I was brought to Downpatrick Magistrates Court. I was before the court on one charge of theft, two forgeries, two for trying to use the forged prescriptions, possession and attempted possession of a controlled drug. The magistrate was fuming. I was given six months in Crumlin Road Prison.

I met plenty of characters in Crumlin. I shared a cell with James, a Loyalist paramilitary. I found it ironic that he wanted to stay in the main part of the prison. He told me he loathed how each faction "claimed" prisoners, which meant that you were brought up in front of the Governor and asked if you belonged to any paramilitary organisation and whether you want to be treated differently. James had been asked this question constantly and he had said he didn't want to be claimed. He would have liked to have been in my position, having no connections with paramilitaries. But after a week in prison he was claimed against his will by the loyalist UVF. He was really aggrieved that he had to move out of our cell and into a different wing. I asked him why he didn't just go along with it. He told me, "Listen, it is hard enough to do time, when you have prison officers to stand up against. Now I have these guys who will tell me on a whim that I have to go on a hunger strike or on a whim that I must refuse to cooperate. I will lose any remission because somebody has decided to make a point – that is why I don't want to be claimed."

The prison was like all the others I had been in before. The first day I took a walk around the exercise yard, and I met a guy who seemed to be affable and friendly. He told me he was a lifer and that he was using his time in prison to study for a degree. I didn't find out what the degree was. But we kept walking along and chatting. He told me how much he looked forward to getting out. Later I told James about my conversation.

"That was one friendly guy," I said.

"Did he tell you why he was inside?"

"No."

"Well," said James, "he murdered his girlfriend and tried to dispose of the body in such a way that people said it was the first case of cannibalism ever in Ireland."

"What?"

"Yeah, this guy had actually eaten part of her up and

put the rest of her back into the ditch where he had killed her . . ."

"But he would be the last person in the world I'd ever think capable of such a thing," I said.

I walked the other way when I saw him in the yard in future.

While I was in prison I got a job in the stores, which in part involved delivering bread to the kitchen. I was on home ground here! The kitchens were the ideal place for anybody to work long term, because you got free food and the best of everything. The stores were the second best job.

I was there about a month, when one day I was bringing bread into the kitchen. The bread was on a big rack of about ten shelves with loaves piled onto each other. The rack was on wheels and I was trying to guide it around the kitchen. I was pushing it very hard and I ran over this guy's toes. He let a yelp out of him. I told him – not very politely – to get out of my way, and pushed past him. About an hour later a guy came up to me and asked me if I realised what I'd done. Apparently I had just told one of the Shankill Butchers to move out of my way in a rather rude manner. I was frightened. The next morning I went up to him and asked, "Would you mind making me a little pouch for my cigarette lighter?" They made money from that. He took my order and made me a pouch, which I took as being a sign that he wouldn't actually kill me!

When my dad died, I was still reeling from Tom's death. I know now, looking back, that I didn't give myself time to grieve for my father. I had been so busy arranging things such as the funeral, doing all the things that I shouldn't have been able to do, but for some reason I could. I still had not grieved properly for either Tom or my dad. But one night in Crumlin Road, it all came to a head. I was lying there in the darkness, on the bunk in my cell, and for no apparent reason I began to weep. I knew as soon as the tears started to flow that that was the first time I truly acknowledged that I *really* missed my dad. I just kept thinking, over and over again, *I miss you*. It was as simple as that. I was finally grieving for him and it was in Crumlin Road Prison – the last place he would have wanted his son to be.

Coming up near Christmas I was due a day release. I was allowed to go out early in the morning, stay overnight at home and come back the next day. I was only out of the prison, walking down the road when I came to a doctor's surgery. I went in, managed to steal a prescription and tried to pass it off in a chemist shop in Lisburn. Some sort of a warning bell in my head must have sounded because I thought twice very quickly and got out of there fairly lively. There I was, out on parole, walking the streets under the warm welcoming seasonal lights, yet I couldn't stop myself from going back to my old habits.

While I was in Crumlin Road Prison, I put my head down to do my six months and I kept off the drugs while I was inside – except for the cigarettes. The prison was completely different from anything I had experienced before, mainly because of the paramilitary influence. Men going about doing their daily jobs in prison knew that they were talking to people who could possibly kill them on the outside. So I think they did their job with a lot more care. One day when we were having some "association" time we all sat focused around the television, watching footage of the aftermath of the Enniskillen bombing. The tension between the IRA and Loyalist prisoners was tangible; it felt like they could have started a mini-war in the prison.

I personally never saw much of the prison violence close up, because I was in a different wing. But I could sense little snippets. Walking along the prison gantry one day I heard a lot of commotion. A prisoner had been called out of the toilets three times by the prison officer. He had refused to come out, so when he came out this sixty-year-old prison officer said, "Hurry up and get into your cell." The prisoner turned around and smacked him. I never saw a sixty-year-old take a twenty-five-year-old down as quick in all my life, but he took him apart.

There was so much tension in there, it only took one little thing to spark things off. You always could sense when something was about to kick off.

In Crumlin Road, I was reacquainted with a guy called Taylor, whom I had shared accommodation with in the hostel in Belfast. I met him in the prison church, and found out he had become a Christian. He kept telling me that I should join him and that I should hear this girl who sang for the prisoners. Her name was Sarah. One Monday night, with nothing better to do, I went along with Taylor. In came Sarah with her guitar and she sat down and sang about the Lord. I remember thinking at the time: *It would be fantastic if I knew what she was singing about.*

Through Taylor, I started to think a wee bit more about God. He would sometimes read the Bible in his cell and ask a few of us to expound on it a bit. We were allowed to do that because the prison officers saw it as worthwhile. Though I didn't make any commitment to God while I was in prison, I began to pray again in a real way. I think that, because I was missing my dad and Tom, I was trying to find a connection. I was trying to get out of the loneliness. I was convinced that when I came out of prison, things would change.

The morning I got out, I asked the prison officers only one thing: could I keep the blue pullover they issued me with? I wanted it as some kind of a souvenir. So I said goodbye to James and I went out dressed in my Crumlin Road pullover. I thought I was cool. I naively thought it was great to have a "badge" that other prisoners on the outside would recognise.

When I got out of Crumlin Road, I was determined to make things different. The prison is approximately fifty yards from the first off-licence – and that's how long my determination lasted. So I went into the first one, bought a bottle of wine and made my way to a place where the winos drank, near City Hall in Belfast. I joined them and I had another bottle. I got the bus home, walked into my mum's and said: *I have to go out now.* I headed straight down to the doctors. I was still a registered drug addict so I got a prescription. That's determination. This way I didn't have to face things.

When I was in prison, everything was done for me. I didn't have to make any decisions, because they were made for me. I didn't have to face up to anything in prison. My world was my cell. I was in my own private rehab centre and it was called prison. When I got out it was a whole different ball game. I was as much a prisoner the moment I hit that off-licence as I had been during those past months. I had dashed my mum's hopes once again. While she never lost faith in me, she would have had high hopes for my recovery but when I came out of Crumlin Road Prison – I'd say she was just hoping. Mum had lost her husband, and her eldest son. She didn't want to believe that she would lose another son.

Chapter 27

Then my probation officer said I needed to get into rehab. I had been in these places a number of times over the years. So I went into Downpatrick Hospital. It soon became crystal clear to me that nobody there had the answer I was looking for. I met a guy who had been sober for nineteen years. I sat down with him, and asked him, "Did you ever have a day when you did not desire the drink and the drugs?" His answer, with tears in his eyes, was, "No, not one single day." And I thought: *Is this it? Is this what they can offer me? Nineteen years fighting every single day against something greater than myself?*

But at least I met people like Gerry, Paddy, Billy, guys who were real, and we had a laugh at the expense of the system. We all knew it was a bit of *craic*, but we took it seriously when we were asked to. When we did group therapy sessions we did not take anybody down; we stood together. It was like prison in that sense. One of the male nurses said that in twenty-five years he had never met a group like us, because we thought we knew it all, asking them questions rather than answering theirs. We would ask: "When you say 'better' what do you mean by 'better'? Do you mean we are all going to come out of here as long as we do over a hundred support meetings every month? Is that really better?" So we gave them lip and a hard time. I suppose that is the nature of addicts, always testing the system, trying to find excuses. Of course, rehab *does* work; it gets you sober. But I have yet to meet a man or woman who has come through it and who can look me straight in the eye and say: *I am free.* I don't believe that it is freedom when a man has to run to meeting after meeting. But if it works for those who are addicted, then that is great.

My feelings now about rehabilitation centres are that they are good and, yes, we could do with more. However, if you take a man off the street and say, *Right, I am going to get you sober and off drugs, and I am going to keep you that way for the next eight weeks*, that is quite easily done. But when that man leaves that rehab centre, the off-licence door is open and the doctor is saying, *Well, here is the drug you want*; or your mates are saying, *Here's some dope.* I believe now that the only way drugs can be one hundred per cent beaten is with Christ. You can only have recovery from addiction with a spiritual connection. That's where God comes in big time. There's no hope without God. Without God it is just a battle, a battle that will continue for the rest of your life. At the end of the day, what is the point in spending your time sober if you have no freedom?

I went along with rehab for a certain amount of time, because I wanted to see if there was any answer in it for me. But within a few weeks, I would always realise that there was no answer. I looked on it as a chance to have a rest. I went in and got my drugs, which were at maintenance level and were reduced as the weeks went on. I would always say: *Maybe, maybe it will work this time*. But I knew deep down that, despite the great efforts of everyone concerned, it wouldn't work. I always knew no one could fill that need that I had and no one could lift the desire I had for these drugs.

I think I knew deep down there was no answer for me in these places but I was willing to give them a shot. At least they would keep me a wee bit straighter for a while. At least I was trying something. When I came out, I didn't think: *Agh well, that didn't work, now I feel even worse*, because it couldn't get any worse. Anyway, if you were to talk to the average druggy or alcoholic about getting out of these places, we all knew that this was just part of our addictive lifestyle. *Oh yer man, he's away to dry out for a few days*. It just became part of my life. Some people get into a whole cycle of it on a regular basis.

When all else fails – when you don't have a place to sleep; when you are facing a court case; when your parents have said, "We can't have you back until you are straight"; when your probation officer says, "I strongly suggest you do this" – those are the times when you say: *I'll have another wee stint in here*.

The only thing that made Downpatrick different was that it finally dawned on me in there that I was addicted. I started to admit that there would never be any change and in fact I couldn't change and no one could help me to change. No doctors, no psychiatrists, no one. Things would go on as before. The only thing that would change was that it would get worse – and that's why injecting seemed like the next logical step, in a totally illogical world.

Chapter 28

I had been drinking very heavily, trying to drown out memories – Tom's death in particular. I went back to Lisburn again, and I got myself a new flat. Every day was the same. I would get up in the morning, reach under the bed for the bottle and have a swig. Then I would get up, make a cup of tea, smoke a few cigarettes and go down to the health centre early, to be near my drugs. I would wait outside until it opened, go in and get my prescription from the doctor. At this stage they would only give me a daily prescription; the doctors would not trust me enough to give me a full prescription in one go. I would then go to the chemist and collect my pills. The chemist, whom I was now on a first-name basis with, would give me a glass of water to help me swallow the pills. Then I would go to the off-licence. I always seemed to have enough money for a cheap bottle of wine. I would trundle back to the flat and sit there on my own, and get even more drunk and stoned out of my head. I had no appetite and lived on bread. I had lost a lot of weight. I didn't care. I was on a mission of self-destruction.

I probably did this for about a year. I would usually go to see my mother about once a week. She was now living in a lovely little bungalow. It became something of a safe haven for me. When I wasn't visiting, I was alone, with my dreams and my wine and my pills. I didn't want to associate with anyone. I didn't want to have a good time. I just wanted to be alone. I was waiting to die. The feelings of emptiness were immense. I just wanted to fill it up for good.

After about a year, a guy who I'd known from years before turned up at the flat unannounced. It was Alan, from the party days when Trish and I had been squatters in Manor Park. He was shocked to see the state of me. Even though he himself was a drug addict and an alcoholic, he couldn't get over seeing me, on a sunny Monday afternoon, sitting inside with a cheap bottle of wine, by myself in the flat, not playing music or watching television. Nothing. Just sitting and staring.

Alan saw something in me that triggered his good nature, because he would not leave me alone until I agreed to come out of the flat. He kept returning and calling for me until eventually, after about a week of pestering me, I did go out. But I was so paranoid as a result of the alcohol and the lonely life that I had been living for the past year. When I got into the first bar, unusually for me, I wanted to run out immediately.

I then found out that Alan was injecting drugs and I asked him if he would introduce me to this new high. Another step up in my drugs career. Another step closer to oblivion.

So one beautiful sunny summer's afternoon, in the back garden of his house in Belfast, I rolled up my sleeve and stuck out my arm.

"Give us it. Is it in yet?"

And that's how I took my first fix of drugs, even though I was frightened of needles.

I began to take a cocktail of drugs. What I got on prescription was dexamphetamine, which was speed, and a thing called tuinal barbiturates or sleepers. I would get a spoon and empty the contents of the capsule of barbiturates onto it. I would then take the tablet of amphetamine and crush it into dust, mix the two in water and then put a little cigarette tip into the middle of it. I would draw up the chemicals through the tip like a filter. So I was taking uppers and downers in the one injection.

When the rush first went up my arm, my eyesight or my awareness of light would go. That was the barbiturates hitting home. Then I would spring into this amphetamine-happy state, mixed with a drunken state from the barbiturates. There were times I would stop using the amphetamines that way, because really it was not necessary. I could swallow those and get the speed high, but the barbiturates were a different story. The difference between injecting and swallowing barbiturates was that if you swallowed two capsules, you had to wait for an hour before you got a buzz, and the buzz was different – it was slow, longer-acting and more moody. If you injected, it went straight to your brain and knocked you for six. With barbiturates I would get the buzz within a split second of the needle being flushed into me. While it didn't last as long that way, the attraction for me was the rush. I got into enjoying the buzz from my hit immediately, right away. I would inject if I was out partying, probably four or five times a night. I would get a hit to last for about two hours. The problem was, I kept increasing the amount on the spoon. Most of these were my prescription drugs, but I also got drugs from other addicts.

The laughable thing was that, when I would inject barbiturates, I still had a sense of pride in the fact that I hadn't injected heroin. It was my way of easing my conscience. Like the guy going down that hill, I hadn't reached the bottom – yet. It was only in recent years, since I started giving my drug education talks, when I realised that in fact the more dangerous of the two is injecting barbiturates, because the overdose line is so fine. So, conscience eased, I continued to take a mixture of amphetamine and barbiturates.

When I injected I would have to find a vein. Over the years my veins would collapse because of all the injecting. But at the time, I knew I had hit a vein when a little bit of blood came into the needle and started to mix with the concoction. I would inject it in. Once that needle was almost empty, I'd pull the plunger out and push it back in again. It was called flushing. It gave me a second rush, a second buzz. The danger was that if I was stoned doing it, I might see the bit of blood but I might push the needle past or through the vein and have a miss and my whole arm or hand, wherever I was injecting, would swell up. Early on, I relied very much on Alan's great ability with the needle. Even when he was in a complete state, so much so that he couldn't even find his finger, he still would never have a miss.

By now my feelings of worthlessness had reached an all-time low. I counted the value of my life by the number of tablets I managed to get from the doctor that week and by the amount I could inject into my body. I wrongly thought that my life was only worth how many drugs and how much money I had at any one particular time. That's why injecting seemed to be a natural sort of progression.

I started injecting at a time in my life when I had finally, totally given up. I no longer knew what it meant to be happy. When I went to pick up my drugs I had a vague sense of excitement, of anticipation. I knew that within a matter of hours I would be smashed, but this was nothing new.

I became an embarrassment to Alan, because he couldn't figure me out. Why would a guy who had all these drugs from the National Health wish them away, saying, *Take them, I am not interested in them?* One day I was in Belfast with Alan. I was out of my head, and I had a hundred dexamphetamine tablets and a hundred barbiturates. I lifted the lids off these two canisters and threw them out onto the street, like I was trying to get them away from me. The very thing that was killing me, I didn't want. But Alan asked what I was doing, and he was going around picking them up off the ground. There was a very overwhelming sadness for me. I couldn't kill myself, but life was just not worth living.

My daily routine changed slightly. I was now going into Belfast to meet Alan, usually in a pub where I drank all the time and I was getting regular amounts of drugs. I still had my prescription drugs and by now the doctor had foolishly trusted me enough to give me a prescription that would last a week or two at a time. I would go on benders with Alan and other hangers-on, which would usually last ten days. On the days I wasn't on a bender I would visit my mother in her bungalow in Lisburn and stay for a couple of days with her, while she fed me and washed me and got me ready to go back out into my world.

During those couple of years with Alan I spent a lot of time in the red light area of Belfast. I got to know people, I began to socialise and I even convinced my mother that I had now got things under control. But of course I didn't tell her that I was injecting. She may have had her suspicions, but she never said anything. On one occasion when I came home from partying in Belfast, I was recovering in her bungalow and she found some needles in the pocket of my duffle coat. I told her that they belonged to a diabetic friend. I told her I had promised to mind them for him and that I had forgotten to give them back at the end of the night. I think my mother accepted that, more out of need than out of belief.

At times we would be sitting in the lovely garden of her wee bungalow, and she would ask me, "Son, why are you wearing a long-sleeved shirt on a sunny day like this?" She never enquired too much, though, because I think she was afraid to have her worst suspicions confirmed.

There would usually be bruising all over my arms and my veins started to collapse a year into the injecting. I

started running out of places on my body to inject into.
The pattern for injecting was that if you were right-
handed you started off with your right arm and you
worked your way down into your hand and then you
went to the left arm and down into your hand. After that
you could even go into your neck or your private parts. I
didn't get as far as that, but I did see other guys doing it.
Eventually, you just run out of veins.

So that was how it was; the pattern was set in concrete.
I got the drugs from the doctor, I got the money from the
dole and I went on a bender with my mates. I had no
relationships with women; that had gone by the board a
long time ago. I would talk to women in pubs, but I was
constantly paranoid. I was starting to suffer from
amphetamine psychosis or "speed madness", even when I
was not on the drugs. Sometimes I got a couple of hours
in the pub where I didn't think people were talking about
me, but generally I was in this paranoid state. I was
always suspicious, always frightened. I was in a cycle and
I couldn't stop the merry-go-round. I thought: *Sure, what
would I do anyway? Where would I go?* If I wasn't sitting
there in the pub with Alan and the others, I'd be sitting in
the flat by myself. This life of injecting and drinking was
the lesser of two evils. And that's just how it went.

I don't think it's a coincidence that, after Tom died, I took
my first fix. Bereavement and depression were all very
much part of it. Before he died, I had never been tempted,
even though over the years I had been in places where
people were injecting. It now seemed to me that life had
long lost its meaning. There had always been that little

spark inside me that would have said, *Maybe one day things will change, maybe there will come a day when I will find some reason to it all.* But that had gone out the window after Tom's death. My anger at God was rich. I constantly battled with Him. I could not understand why He didn't take me instead of my beloved brother Tom.

The injecting seemed to appeal to me because I was inflicting an injury on myself, punishing myself. I cut my wrists on a couple of occasions. I know it was attention-seeking, because nobody ever tried to kill themselves with a two-inch razor blade.

I was now living in a council flat in a high-rise block in Lisburn. One morning I woke up in the flat by myself, took a drink from the bottle of alcohol beside the bed and got dressed. But I deliberately stayed in my bare feet. I knew the gangway outside the flat was strewn with pieces of smashed broken glass bottles. I walked out my front door, over the jagged edges and back into the flat with bits of glass sticking out of my feet. There was blood pouring from the soles.

Why did I do that? I was so lonely, that wee bit of pain gave me something to concentrate on for a while and brought me out of myself.

After a couple of years, Alan and I went our separate ways. He couldn't stick my paranoia, because it ruined every evening that we went out. I was always creating these scenes with people. So he told me to get a life, and I went my own way and he went his. I drew in on myself again. Apart from the odd occasion, I stopped fixing.

Chapter 29

It was now the early 1990s and I was in my late thirties. As I said, I had drawn back into myself again. I spent most of my time with a guy called Lenny. Lenny was another alcoholic, and he also had a psychological problem. He had a flat down the road from where I lived. We started drinking together. He would occasionally use and take some of my drugs.

I was back in the routine of standing outside the chemist shop at half past eight every morning to get my supply of medicine for the day. I shuffled between that and the off-licence and my own flat. My flat was filthy; you wouldn't put a dog in it. It had a bed and a cooker, and that was really it. There were no curtains on the window, but it didn't matter because nobody was going to see me anyway.

My anger at God was rife. One cold and starry October night it all came to a head. I had sunk to the bottom of my despair. I was in my flat and decided to get out onto the window ledge. It was only about nine inches in width. I was balancing on my tiptoes in my bare feet, hanging onto the sliding window, with just two fingers holding me back from letting go. I shook my fist up at the dark night sky and shouted, "God! If you're there? I just want you to know I hate you for taking my brother!"

I listened, but there was nothing except the sounds of front doors slamming, cars driving along the road below. I waited and waited for what seemed like an eternity. I felt the cold night close in on me. I began to shiver and suddenly I saw myself as I was, trying to take my own life, trying to punish God. Meekly I crawled back in off the ledge, into the warm flat.

I continued to self-harm. I was hacking into my arms, sometimes even when I was stoned, using razor blades. I started thinking more and more about overdoses. I would find myself waking up in the Lagan Valley Hospital with the doctor shaking his head, saying, "You really shouldn't be alive, you have taken so much this time."

I lost a lot of weight. I probably weighed about nine stone at best, which is not good for somebody who is six feet tall.

The one thing that kept me alive was my mother, because I was calling in to her once a week for a couple of days, so I would be fed and cleaned up and able to keep this semblance of respectability about me. She would say, "When you are after doing these things to yourself, come into the house and I will bathe you, and wash your clothes and feed you. I'll allow you to stay in the box room for a few days."

It was a routine. I would be released back into my flat, clean-shaven, and she would usually have given me a new pair of jeans and some other items of clothes, things like that. She would load me up with food parcels to take back, intended to last me a few weeks. I would get into the flat, unpack, and I would see she had slipped in a wee New Testament down the sides of the parcel. I'd be stoned, and I'd send it flying across the room. I think I had more Bibles in that flat than I had dust.

My mum, all her life, had believed that Christ was the answer, and she never lost her faith. After we children were born and were brought to Sunday school, my mum, along with my dad, would be the driving force. The best way I can describe her is as a prayer-warrior. When she lost her son Tom and then her husband just a year after that – a lesser woman would have gone insane. Mum was then told she had cancer, and she had to do battle with that on her own while I was in Crumlin Road Prison. During those six months I was inside, my mum had been to visit me with my aunt Belle, and had never once said anything. But she came out the other side of that, her faith still strong, while I came out only to begin to inject.

My mum knew by now that there was very little hope, if any, of me ever changing. She used to keep the door open for me, as wide as circumstances would allow. In other words, if I was in any reasonable state, I could come into her house and stay there. If I wasn't, I needed to stay in my own flat.

Unknown to me, but not unknown to God, for years

she had been visiting different churches every week. She would get on a bus or a train, take taxis a few times or get lifts from friends. One night she walked four miles in a pouring thunderstorm to get to one particular church. When she arrived, the gates were locked, so she stuck a note between the railings and walked the four miles back home again. That note simply read: *Please pray for my son, Jackie, a drug addict. From a loving mother.*

My mother approached everybody and anybody. Desperation has no denomination. Her Catholic friends, her Protestant friends, all of whom were believers – they were the ones she asked directly. She would take little pieces of paper into the church, sit at the back, and write her prayer down. Then she would take a couple of coins out of her bag, wrap the notes around them, put the coins into a box or onto a plate – anywhere they might be found. She would even leave the little paper petitions behind on trains and buses, anywhere she went to during the normal course of her day. She was looking for prayers from as many as possible and that is, I believe, how God heard her cry.

I used to walk around Lisburn wearing my hardy duffle coat, even in the summer. By this stage, my paranoia had grown to epic proportions. I would be hiding the head of a hatchet in my pocket and the shaft of it up my sleeve. I also kept this hatchet under my pillow at night. I was convinced that people were out to kill me. I wasn't carrying it to attack anyone; I wasn't a violent person. I was carrying it for protection, against imagined enemies.

I used to sit looking out my window for long stretches at a time, watching the cars driving past my block of flats, a pen and paper in my hands so I could write down their number plates. I was totally convinced that these cars were being used by people who were scouting me out to kill me. After, I would go down to the chemist to take my pills; I would get to feel good for about an hour. The rest of the time this sheer state of paranoia would take over.

I would stay very much on my own. Occasionally I would spend a bit of time with family or hang out with a guy called Harry. (Harry later died in a police station in England in a drunken stupor.) There was nothing remarkable in my life. My twenty-four hours went something like this. A cold evening, at the end of a bender on drink and drugs, I'd stumble into my mum's bungalow. I would be getting ready for the next morning when I would get my prescription from the doctors and money off the dole. I'd have a meal with my mum. I'd watch a bit of television, go to bed at about ten o'clock and not sleep very well because my stomach would be twisted with nerves – thinking that the next morning I'd get my drugs and my money. I'd think: *This week is going to be so much different from last week.* I'd get up in the early morning, wash and shave, and go down to the health centre, where I'd get my drugs. It didn't open until half past eight but I'd be outside it at half past seven, walking up and down. Just because I wanted to be close to my drugs, even though I couldn't get them.

At opening time, the receptionist would arrive. I would follow her up the stairs. She would know what I was there for. Most times she didn't even take her coat off. She would just hand me my prescription with a look of disgust. What would she know? I'd cross the street to my usual chemist. The pharmacist would arrive in his jeep. He would know what I was there for. He would pull up the shutters of the shop. There would be little conversation, maybe a "Good morning, Jackie". He would take my prescription. I would follow him into the shop. He would go behind the counter, not taking his coat off either. He would open up the cabinet where they kept all the dangerous drugs. He would take out seven dexamphetamine; four barbiturates; two Tagamet for my stomach because I would have burned the lining off it with drinking; and two Valium to take the edge off it all. He would hand me this mix of tablets and a wee glass of water, and I'd knock them back in one. He knew I wouldn't be patient enough to wait the five minutes while he would make up the rest of my prescription.

After that, I would cross the road to the post office and get my dole money. I would go on up to the off-licence and buy a carry-out of beer, not because I really wanted it, but because I'd be hoping my mates would visit and spend a bit of time with me that day. I knew they wouldn't call unless they got a free drink. At two o'clock in the afternoon, the first knock would come at the door of my flat. The mates had arrived to drink my drink, smoke my dope, take some of my pills.

At half past three in the morning, I would be sitting by myself. The mates would be gone, maybe smashed the window of the flat before they left. Early morning, I would be walking around the estate by myself. I would see a milkman delivering milk, and wonder: *If I spoke to him, would he speak to me or would he be like the rest of the world? Would he just walk past?* I would remember myself as a boy of fifteen, who had so many plans for his life. I would think: *Oh well, maybe next week will be better than this.*

There was never any chink in the darkness. But I do remember some kindnesses along the way. One day, for some reason, I was refused my drugs in the health centre. The doctor would not entertain me at all. I sat down in the foyer and began to weep. Suddenly I felt an arm going around my shoulder. It was the receptionist, a lady whom I had hardly taken any notice of before. She asked me: "Would you like a cup of tea or coffee?" I said I would, and she went and got me a cup of tea. She asked why I was crying, and I told her, whining like a baby, "I can't get my drugs, I can't get my drugs." She sat on and chatted to me for a while and after a short time she mentioned the name of the Lord Jesus Christ. That was the first mention I had heard of Him since my days in Crumlin Road Prison.

Around three o'clock one morning, I was sitting cross-legged in my big empty flat when I looked across the room and spotted something jutting out from under the sideboard. It was one of the New Testaments that my mother used to pack into my bag. It could have been lying there for two months, after I had thrown it there, and it was covered in dust. But for no apparent reason, this time, I crawled under and pulled it out, blew the dust off, got back up on the bed and said out loud: "Well, God, if you are there, have you anything to say?" And I opened it up and read: *"For do you not know that even at this moment you are being formed in the temple for God?"* I closed the book and I thought: *If that were only true – that there was a purpose to the loneliness and emptiness I feel right now – then I could put up with it.*

One night, a year later, my life was saved.

Chapter 30

It was the 18th of August 1994. My mother had to go into the Royal Victoria Hospital in Belfast for an eye operation, to get a cataract removed. I knew this was not a serious operation, but at her age, every operation is serious. I had been on one of my ten-day drink and drugs benders. At a quarter past eight in the morning, when she was getting ready to go, I called into her house on my way to get my drugs. I was going to be a good son that morning; I was going to see my mum before she went into hospital, to wish her all the best for her operation.

I went into the kitchen. She said, "Go and sit yourself down and have a cup of tea."

"I can't, Mum. I have a bit of business to do."

She knew what the business was. It was urgent for me to get to the chemist to get my drugs. She said, "I have the kettle on, I have the taxi ordered for nine to take me to Belfast."

Come on now, anybody would have given a woman like that fifteen minutes of their time, wouldn't they? No. If you'd messed around with drink and drugs for as long as I had, as you got older, if you got older, the time you'd have for your drink and drugs would grow and your relationships would fall apart. Mum went up to that hospital alone and frightened. I got my drugs and brought them home. I took my drugs.

It was eight o'clock the next evening. I had no drink, no drugs and no money left. I was by myself as usual, walking up the town. It was a mild evening. I was thinking about going into my flat, but I didn't want to because of the state of it; it was stinking. I wondered to myself if my brother Raymond was out of the house. He would normally call to mum's house every day. Had he gone to walk my mum's wee dog? If he was out with the dog while she was in hospital, then he may have left the side gate open. Maybe I could slip into the bungalow and into the wee box room and get a good night's sleep?

The brother had the side gate locked, so I climbed up over it and I saw that the door to the kitchen was open. I went in, praying to get into the box room, to get undressed and into bed. I wanted to get to sleep as soon as possible, because if Raymond came back with my mum's dog, to lock up the house and if he had found me awake, he might actually have said it was time for me to get out once and for all.

I was looking for a good night's sleep; that's all I was looking for. I lay down and fell into a sleep. At four o'clock in the morning, I woke up in a very strange way.

I was actually praying as I woke, and I hadn't prayed for years. I mean, what was the point in praying? God was deaf. But the same prayer was coming out, "Father, Father, please don't let me die like this, don't let me die like this."

Why was I praying like this? I was praying to get out of bed. As soon as I tried to get out, my legs buckled beneath me. It was barbiturate poisoning. I knew the symptoms because I had it so many times before. I was physically dying. I personally believed this. It was a much different sensation from anything I had felt before. I was waiting for a grand mal seizure to take me over at any moment. I knew what I needed to do: get to the phone, call for an ambulance, get myself into Lagan Valley Hospital, get a saline drip put into me and get my system cleaned out.

I crawled into the living room and lay on the sofa. But there was a presence in the room. It was as real as you are now, reading this. The presence was Jesus Christ. Do you know what the Son of God did? He turned the pages of my memory showing me how many times, even when I was a wee boy, that he had called me. He showed me all the times I had used drugs and said, *"Jackie, you've tried everything else, would you not try me? Jackie, you've done that now, would you not come to me?"*

I said, "Just heal me, Lord."

For about an hour and a half I tried to make a deal with God. *If you do this, I will do that,* I said to Him. The power of addiction was so strong that, even with the presence of Christ Himself in that room, what did I do? I tried to make a deal. "Lord, I know you are here, but if you'd just heal me, I'll cut down on my drugs, I'll be a better son to my mother, I'll even go to church once in a while." But I realised that God didn't make deals. There could be no deals.

At half past five that morning the presence of God left me. I had abandoned all hope. I just sat down and wept for the next hour and twenty minutes. I knew I had missed an opportunity that I was certain would never come again. I knew for the first time, for the only time in my life, that there was no point ever again calling out *"God help me"* because He may not listen to me.

It was almost seven o'clock in the morning and I was still crawling around on the floor. The poison had got so deeply into my body that by now the only parts of me working were my elbows. I pulled myself across the carpet. I was going to phone for an ambulance, but it was only by the grace of God that I was going to do that. As I reached for the phone, it suddenly started ringing.

"Hello, Mr Burke?"

"Yes?"

"It's the Royal Victoria Hospital. We're concerned. You mother has had her operation successfully, but she wants to sign herself out early to come home to you. Now, will you be there to meet her when she arrives home?"

"Yes, I'll be there."

But I knew I would have to get into hospital myself. How could I be there for my mother?

I thought, *One day, I'm gonna die and when that day comes, I'll never see my mother again. She's assured of heaven but I have no idea where I'm going.*

It was just that wee thought – no great leap of faith – just that wee thought that triggered me. It turned me around. It made me call out, more in desperation than in faith, "Lord Jesus, I'm begging you, would you please come back and just give me one last chance? If you do, I promise you, no deals this time. You can take my life and do what you want with it."

At ten minutes to seven I could not have taken a few simple steps by myself. At ten past seven the feeling came back into my legs and I was up walking, standing, cleaning the place up, getting ready for my mother coming home. Healed and totally delivered from the so-called life I once had.

If you were to meet me now, you would not be looking at a rehabilitated addict. You would be looking at someone who had taken the hand of Christ. When He sets you free, you're free. When the Son of God heals you, you are healed.

Chapter 31

I waited for quite some time at the front window looking out for mum's taxi. Eventually it parked outside. I opened the front door, and saw mum standing there with the door keys in her hand. She glanced up at me, and seemed relieved to see me looking and sounding sober. I took her arm and we walked into the kitchen. I put the kettle on and made her a cup of tea. She sat down.

"I have something to tell you," I said.

"Don't tell me, son – the police have been around."

I laughed at the notion, it sounded absurd. I leaned across the table and took her hand.

"No, mum," I replied. "I have become a Christian."

Mum looked very puzzled. I think she could hardly dare hope that the words her son was speaking were in fact the truth. After all these years, these words were the answer to her prayers.

"Really, son?"

"Yes, from now on everything is going to be different. No more drugs, no more deals. No more drink."

She simply said: "Thank God."

Four days went past. I was physically healed. The very least I should have experienced over that time was a grand mal seizure, a huge epileptic-type fit, which I always had with withdrawals. The least that should have been done for me was that I should have been hospitalised, and over two months brought down gradually from the drugs.

I didn't break a sweat. I didn't need an aspirin. I didn't need any drugs. I didn't wake up with a halo, of course, but I allowed prayer to give me strength and to hold on.

Inside, though, there was still that burning desire, that voice inside my head, saying, *Maybe one day I'll go back to the drugs. Come on, don't be silly. You'll never be able to do without them.* During those four days, each morning was the same. The first thought that came to me was: *Get to the chemist – get your script and get the drugs.* The drugs were still the centre of my life. I thought about them all the time. I believed that if I didn't take them I would have a fit. But I was taking a leap of faith in God. It was like learning to swim and letting go. Even though the negative thoughts were pounding my brain, underneath it all I knew God had done something real with me – even if my body could not explain it.

I spent those initial days pacing the floor at home, almost daring to be healthy, waiting for the first signs of something to go wrong. Yet, at the same time, I was praying, praying like I had never done before. I kept on calling out to the Lord, saying: "Lord, help me to hold on."

I started to read the Bible. I hadn't read it closely for years, and I turned a page in St John's Gospel and came to Chapter 10, Verse 10, where Christ said: *"The thief comes only to steal, kill and destroy; I have come that you may have life, and have it to the full."* When I read that verse, on that fifth day, something really hit me. I thought: *You know what, He has not only healed me physically, but He can actually take the desire for these things from me.*

On the sixth day, after thinking about that verse, meditating on it, I was walking my mum's dog around the local park. I was halfway around when I just cried out to the Lord again. I knew that I could not walk out of that park feeling the same way I had walked into it, because things were getting harder and harder. So I called and called out to the Lord. I said, "Lord, I thank you for healing me physically, but you have to take this *desire* for drugs from me." And I actually quoted that verse back to the Lord: "It says, You will give me life and life to the full – that's a life in abundance. It says, the thief will come to destroy. Well, I know all about him. He has taken my daughter, my brother, my father, my happiness. You say you can give me life, life in abundance – thank you for healing me physically, but now Lord, you have got to take this desire from me."

Halfway around that park I felt a real sense of God's Holy Spirit. I walked out a free man.

As I write this, that was nearly thirteen years ago, and I have never looked back – never desired drugs, never relapsed. I started to read the Bible every day, and all I wanted was to have a nice quiet life with my mother.

When God is in your heart, things start happening very quickly. About nine or ten weeks later, I needed to enquire about getting my driving licence. Years before I had lost my licence, because one day I was driving a van around town and I was spotted by a doctor who knew I was a registered drug addict. So at the time the Department of the Environment had told me I had to surrender my licence or go to court to fight for it. I knew the only real option was to let them have it. Looking back, I am glad that happened to me. That doctor possibly saved not only my life, but other people's lives, because I was in danger of causing a serious accident.

But this time around I was a changed man. I phoned an inspector at the Department of the Environment. I told him what had happened to me and he said: "You know, not that I doubt you, but we have to get some proof of it." He told me I needed to get a full medical, so I did.

The doctor walked in with my results. He was completely baffled. My liver: perfect; my kidney function: perfect . . . everything, even my cholesterol, was perfect. The doctor just shook his head and said, "You just shouldn't have these results. Not with the life you have led."

I went back to the Department of the Environment. They had a medical committee meeting about it. They looked at the results, and came back to tell me, "Look, you have got to talk to a psychiatrist and convince him that what you are telling us has happened."

I was scheduled to meet a psychiatrist for four weeks of interviews. Three weeks into it he said, "Well, Mr Burke, there is no point in you coming again. After all, the facts speak for themselves."

I got my driving licence.

I do believe what happened to me was a miracle. Absolutely no question about it. What's more, I can even prove it. It isn't just the medical reports that back this up – there is the fact that I am still here, still living and breathing, all those years later.

In those early days, I began to call myself a Christian – someone who is a follower of and a believer in Christ. So that is what I became. People have asked me how I would describe those early days, my miracle. My answer: "I was dragged kicking and screaming in protest into the Kingdom of God through the prayers of my mother and the love of Jesus Christ." And many people, like my mother and others, continued to pray, year in, year out, for me. People I had never met before who were contacted through friends had all been praying, unknown to me, for years.

I caught up with some of those people who had never lost faith in me. I wrote a letter to Dave Burnel in London and told him about what had happened. I also asked him to forgive me. I was wracked with guilt over all the bad things I had done and the people I had hurt. Dave had got married and his wife wrote back immediately telling me that the day my letter arrived, Dave was over the moon. He had taken the letter and run to her saying, "He's done it! He's done it!" Dave himself wrote and told me he had forgiven me long ago and that he had been praying for me and always would. He still is to this day.

I thought about that receptionist at the Health Centre who had been kind to me when I was refused my drugs. One day, I walked up to that same counter in the foyer in a different way. The duffle coat and the old clothes were gone. I was wearing a suit, a shirt and a tie, a marked difference. As I came towards the counter the look on that woman's face was priceless. She wore a smile a mile wide. She jumped out of her seat and when I said I had become a Christian she said, "Well, thank God!" I said, "I'm just going up to have a word with the doctor," and she said, "Fair play to you!" When I went in to see the doctor, I told him I was not down for drugs and I would never be back for drugs of that sort. I don't really know if he took it on board.

One night, I went out to a church and there was a singer on a platform. It was Sarah, the woman whom I had heard singing while I was in prison. I hadn't spoken to her in the prison, but she saw me sitting in the church and recognised me. When she finished singing to the Lord, she ran straight to me, threw her arms around me and said, "It is great to see you, now that you are really free." She was one of the many people who had been praying for me and I had known nothing about it.

Of course, there were times when I was tempted to go back on drink and drugs, especially in the early years when things got tough. Temptation was never far away. I was offered more drugs in my first year as a Christian than I had ever been offered before.

While most of my old friends were delighted for me

that I had found God, others went out of their way to test me to see how "real" it all was. One day, walking down Lisburn town, I spotted a local dealer. For that split second I was numb; it was like a terrible fear had taken hold of me. I was afraid I would not be strong enough to walk past him without asking for some drugs. I prayed: "Lord, take him out of my way; I am not strong enough yet." Suddenly he checked his pockets as though he had forgotten something, turned and walked off. I was very humble and grateful to God for that. I was like a baby holding His hand, learning to walk all over again. Another day I saw this guy sitting drinking a pint of beer out in the sunshine and I looked over and I thought, for a fleeting second: *That looks nice.* But then I thought: *Wise up.*

The second year I had an experience that really brought home where I had come from. I had started to do some drug counselling, trying to help others get off drink and drugs. I had been counselling a guy called Rob and one day I found him in an awful state with drink. I was really upset; I had put about six months work into this guy, and was disgusted that he seemed to be falling back.

I left Rob's house and got into my car, still upset. My next appointment was with a guy called Gary. Gary was blind, and when he opened the door and I saw that he was out of his head on prescription drugs, I thought: *This is the worst day of my Christian counselling life.* I said to Gary before I went that I was going to say a wee prayer. As I got up to go, he asked me to come into the bedroom because there was something he wanted me to see. The nerves in my stomach were still twisted from the disappointment with Rob – and now I was standing in this blind man's bedroom and he put into the palm of my hand a big tube with about one hundred Valium tablets in it. And in a flash Satan was on my shoulder, saying: *Take a couple, he is blind, he'll never know. Come on, you're upset; God wouldn't blame you if you took two Valium. Come on, help yourself.*

I threw them back into his hand and said I had to go. I jumped into the car and got out of the place. I drove around the corner and pulled into a garage. The sweat just came pouring out of my forehead. I had been so tempted, but I thanked God for helping me to get through it. It shook me, but looking back I realise that only God allows you to be tempted just beyond what you can stand. I was brought to the edge that day, but it strengthened me. He took that temptation and turned that around.

As time went on, a lot of people insisted that when I became a Christian I'd have this honeymoon period where I would be filled with enthusiasm, but that this was only temporary and would then fade. But for me it had been, and still is, the total opposite: I love God more today than I did thirteen years ago. His love for me has not changed. I just can't do anything without being completely thankful. I should not have any of this, I did not earn it; it was given to me and I just thank God that He was the one who gave it. I've never been tempted to go back.

Chapter 32

In the beginning after my transformation, I was a bit zealous about my beliefs. I would go around wearing a suit and holding the Bible under my arm. My mother was proud, to say the least! I attended a meeting once a week, where a lot of people like myself got together. Many who went to these meetings came from backgrounds involving alcohol and drugs but who, like me, had found Christ. We would say a few prayers and try to find a message in our lives from Jesus. They were a good bunch to be with, and I was involved in their Christian counselling course. They helped me to grow in faith and to be strong. After less than a year with them, I met my wife Hilary.

We were introduced through mutual friends and we didn't gel together. As Hilary would say, I was a "self-righteous, arrogant Mr Filofax Man". On the other hand, I would have described her as "obnoxious and stubborn". Our first conversation went like this:

Me: "Do you know many people here?"

Her: "No."

Me: "Are you enjoying the evening?"

Her: "Yeah – it's fine."

Me: "Would you like to get something to eat?"

Her: "No, not really."

Me: "You're not very talkative, are you?"

Her: (Deathly stare) "No."

And that was about it – everything was just "fine". As you can guess, we took an instant dislike to each other, but everyone else swore they saw something going on.

I met Hilary on and off over the next few months. We bumped into each other at various friends' houses and at some Christian events. We both got involved in helping to run a drop-in centre and during the spare time there we began to chat. I actually managed to get more than a few "fines" from her! And as time went on, we formed a friendship.

I decided to ask Hilary out for a meal. I told her we needed to discuss a mutual friend who was having some problems. While this was the truth, I also wanted an opportunity to spend more time with her. Up until then, we had just been friends, in and out of each other's company at various times. But during that meal I decided I was going to tell Hilary how I felt about her. I was really nervous. Apart from anything else, there was quite an age gap between us and our upbringings were quite different. I had no idea how Hilary was going to react – so I went for the safe option.

"You know, I like you."

"Aww, that's lovely. I like you too."

"No, but I *really* like you."

At this point Hilary almost choked on her meal. Not the response I was looking for. After a few questions and answers we drove out to Newcastle. It was to be the first of our many visits to that beautiful part of Northern Ireland. We sat on the beach and talked for hours.

I had known Hilary for six months. The parents of someone in my counselling group, which I was running at the time, were jewellers. Being the crafty sod that I was and without saying anything to Hilary, I asked them, "Would you let me borrow three or four of your engagement rings – just until Hilary picks one?" They helped out. So one night I had four engagement rings burning holes in my pocket when I went to pick Hilary up from work! It was all top secret.

After I picked Hilary up, we headed out to mum's bungalow. My mum was the only one who knew about it, but she was also keeping it a secret until I had actually proposed. We usually spent a bit of time there having coffee and a chat before we'd go out for the night. But that evening, when we arrived at the house, mum was not thinking – she thought I had already asked Hilary. I was the first into the house and mum said, as soon as we came through the door, "Well, what did she say?" I groaned, "Ah mum!" Hilary said, "What was that?"

Nothing more was said until later that night when I asked her properly. Hilary, reluctantly, said, "Yes". And I do mean reluctantly. She said, after I proposed, "Well, I have to think about it." I said, "Would you even wear the ring on your finger?" She put it on the right hand

and then after a week or two she changed it over to the left.

When I first became a Christian, I had no interest in women *per se*, because my whole focus was on God. At the time, I decided that I was going to work for God for the rest of my life. Nothing and no one was going to stop me in the pursuit of being the "perfect" Christian. He knew that I wasn't listening to Him, because I had become almost fanatical about my faith. Faith and fanaticism can be a good mix if you are doing the right thing, but I was unwilling to listen to God's spirit at certain times. I was finding it difficult to get that balance between love and zeal. As a drug addict, I had always gone that extra mile to get that higher high. I did whatever it took. And now that I was a Christian, I brought that same single-mindedness with me. God eventually brought Hilary into my life to level me out.

As she said, I *was* Mr Filofax Man – the man in the suit, shirt and tie, with the Bible under my arm. A mother's dream! I thought I had to dress like this to show everyone how serious I was about being a Christian. But then Hilary offered suggestions – jeans and t-shirt became my new "wardrobe". And for a while, I had a look to die for! I had the two best fashion experts in the world – mum and Hilary. But mum would hide the jeans from Hilary and Hilary would hide the ties. It was comical at times.

But it wasn't just the outward signs that Hilary affected in me. She also shared with me her sense of humour and I learned how to laugh again. So in that sense I wouldn't be the person that I am today without her. I wouldn't be as relaxed.

As to whether we made a perfect match, I would say we are opposites in some ways. I can be impulsive where Hilary would weigh things up a lot more. I would be discerning in some ways, she would be in others. I suppose we just balance each other out. Hilary can see through camouflage more easily than I can. Maybe at times I don't want to see through it but she will always think of the "what if" syndrome.

Chapter 33

Of course, by this time Kathy and I had officially divorced. So Hilary and I were on our way to getting married. We went through the usual stuff that goes along with all that territory. I had to get to know her father and mother. Thankfully we get along really well and they have always been there for us, like my own family.

Hilary and I "tied the knot" in early 1997 in Lisburn Cathedral Church. Even up until the very last moment, I was not sure if she was going to turn up. But she did and it was a wonderful marriage ceremony. The Canon gave us his blessing. We had signed all the papers in the registry office before that. During the blessing, the minister gave us two wee teddy bears and asked us to keep them all our married life. Hilary and I looked at each other; we didn't know what was going on. But then he started to read a passage out of the Bible; it went along the lines of "to bear one another's burdens". We laughed and indeed the teddy bears were to prove a great reminder to us down through the years. It was a very laid-back affair. Raymond and Hilary's sister Caroline were our two witnesses. Hilary's cousin Barbara took the photographs and a mutual friend prepared a buffet for everyone in the church hall. After the reception we travelled to Kerry for our honeymoon, and when we returned, we moved in to our new home in Lisburn.

When I look back, I see we had an almost child-like delight in making a home. We were like a couple of teenagers, stripping wallpaper, slapping on paint (and I mean slapping). My DIY skills are limited, so it was like the house that Jack built!

As I was coming out of that life that I once had, the simple things like grocery shopping, sharing breakfast or just going for a walk became a delight. These were the mundane things that people take for granted, but were amazing to me. Hilary's infectious humour had now taken hold of me, and it came in handy when times got difficult.

Hilary had been told years earlier that she would have trouble conceiving without medical help. However, God is a God of surprises – our son Matthew was born on 30 December 1997, much to our utter delight. I watched Matthew come into the world and I cradled him in my arms as the song "Perfect Day" played in the background. I just kept looking at him in wonder. Now we have also added Rachel, born in 2001, and Jonathan, born in 2006, into our little family.

In the early days of our marriage I was doing bits of work here and there with church groups and youth groups and the like. We did come close to the wire financially on a few occasions. Looking back at it, we had what some people might have said was an unreasonable belief that God was going to use us. I felt I had some sort of calling, but I wasn't sure what it was. I was married with a child. We were barely surviving. Our families helped us out with a few quid and we also got some money from doing the work with groups and community centres, where I gave my little talks. But there was nothing really solid.

We were scrambling about, because I did not have a "real" job. I travelled on one occasion to a place up the north. Hilary and I were completely broke and I said, "At least I am giving a talk tonight; maybe I will get twenty pound." So I travelled all the way up the country to this little town in the middle of a remote peninsula. I finally found the place and stood in front of a room full of people, where I emptied my heart to them. And the guy in charge walked up to me after the meeting. He had a little parcel which he handed to me, saying, "Thanks for coming." It was heavy for such a small parcel. I said to myself, there's probably no money but at least there might be a nice present and that would cheer Hilary up when I'd come home. I smiled politely and thanked the man. I was barely around the corner in the car, when I stopped and ripped open the paper. It was a box of screwdrivers. And I thought: *A box of screwdrivers!* This was crazy. I got home – and, do you know what, the value of laughter that Hilary and I got out of that was worth so much more than twenty pounds.

A year later, the same guy rang me back and asked me to come up again. On that occasion he presented me with an Aled Jones CD. I couldn't wait to go back the next year to see what we would get!

There were times during that first year when we didn't have a bean. I remember searching down the back seat of the car to scrape out a few bob to get some money together so I could buy something for the house. It was tough, but we had this belief that God was going to move me to talk to people in some way.

You can call it madness, but I went down to the dole and told them I wanted to sign off. The girl asked me "Where are you going to work?"

"I'm going to work in faith," I told her.

She looked at me. "Is that in Belfast?"

When I explained what I meant she said: "You really need to think about that."

I promised her I would give it some thought. She was really begging for me to stay on the dole, because she didn't see the sense in it. The next day I went back and I said I would sign off. She said I would lose my contributions towards my pension. I said that the Lord could come back the next day, so why would I need a pension?

I know it sounds crazy, but when I walked out of the dole office, I wasn't on the street five seconds when I heard somebody call to me. I turned around and it was a guy I knew whom I hadn't seen in a long, long time. He walked up and said it was great to see me. He shook my hand, and in his hand was a twenty pound note.

I thought then that that was confirmation from God

that things would work out all right. But we still had to be patient and to wait and see what would happen. At one stage I went for a job interview as a care assistant. I had made up my mind that if I got that job I would go down that road. I was halfway through the interview when I felt an unreasonable guilt on my shoulder. I truly felt that I should not have been in that place. This was not what God wanted. When I came out of that interview I told Hilary I would not be applying for any more jobs until God had spoken. Hilary turned around and agreed. Once we were settled on the idea that this wilderness could go on for another year, things started to change.

I began by writing to as many doctors as I could, trying to tell them that I felt the policy of handing pills out at random was very wrong. Many had a service that provided drugs on a constant basis and they were easily accessible. But not one doctor wrote back to me. I do understand that most doctors are doing their best dealing with addicts within the remits of the Health Service. Maybe if we had more drug rehabilitation centres and aftercare it would take away the burden from the ordinary GP and break the cycle that most addicts initially fall into.

The idea of working in schools and colleges came about. One day, Hilary and I were walking around Wallace Park in Lisburn. I said to her, "You know, I really feel that God might want me in schools." She said, "Funny, that is what I am thinking too." We rushed home that day with the idea of sending off letters to schools. But between one thing and another we didn't get around to it.

A year later, we were pushing Matthew around the same park. I said to Hilary, "Remember last year we were planning to send letters to the schools? Well, let's do it." So I borrowed an old typewriter. We spent three days typing individual letters, going through all the schools in the Yellow Pages. I never knew there were so many saints in Northern Ireland!

I needed money for stamps and envelopes. So I prayed to the Lord and I went and talked to my mum. She gave me sixty pounds from her pension and we bought the envelopes and the stamps and sent off the letters.

What we didn't know, but what God obviously had known, was that, if we had sent the letters in the first year we had the vision for the work, most of the letters would probably have been thrown in the bin. But a year later was the ideal time, because it was the first year in which drug education became a compulsory part of the curriculum in every school in Northern Ireland.

Before we sent out any letters, a teacher at one of the local schools in Lisburn invited me to speak to his RE class. It was a learning curve for me. I had thirty-five minutes to fill. What was I going to do? I just started to tell them my life story. Very quickly I could see the effect that it had on them. I knew this had to be an integral part of anything I was to do in the future in schools. I got feedback from them and that gave me a good sense of what I should say to the students.

Roger had been great, he had helped me to learn my trade, so to speak, and on numerous occasions, sometimes three or four days in a row, I would take the various RE class years. Roger wrote me out a lovely reference. I also got the head of the Drug Squad in Belfast to write me one. He had heard about me and had asked me to speak at a local town meeting where a young boy had died because of his abuse of ecstasy. He hadn't died on the ecstasy – he had blown his head off with a shotgun because it had driven him to depression. But I remember him saying to me, "You are the future of what we are trying to do." A psychiatrist friend also wrote a letter. So I had three references.

Then a local minister gave us his house to use for a couple of weeks. So we sent the letters and we went off for a holiday to the coast. We were just praying our hearts out. *Lord, if this is for us, let us know.* Halfway through the holiday, I couldn't stick it. I drove home and switched on the answering machine. I listened to messages from people calling from school after school, asking me to come to talk.

The doors had opened. That was the beginning of the work.

I learned very quickly that all I needed to do was to show my heart, because God would do the rest. In the letters I said I would like to visit their school, talk to the pupils about drug education and to give it a different slant.

The first school to respond was in Enniskillen. They had the honour of having tutored Oscar Wilde. The gates were about fifteen or twenty feet high, encrusted in black and gold, and there was a driveway leading up to what can only be described as a Victorian mansion. This was the façade of the school. I arrived about forty minutes early, I was so psyched up. I got out of the car with the little case I had for carrying all my essentials. I began to stroll around the gravelled car park and look out past the beautiful lawns and the well-kept flowerbeds. For a moment, it reminded me of Lagham Manor.

I got to a bench and sat down. I decided it would be a good idea to say a few prayers, so I started praying and praying. *What am I going to do here, Lord? What am I doing here?* Of course, I had some idea what I was going to do, but I had no idea how it was going to go down. Finally, I was met by a Mr McPhillips, who had a flowing black gown and wore a watch-chain across his waistcoat. He was the archetypical professor. He brought me inside and I rabbited on, saying what I hoped I was going to do, until halfway through he said, "Take it easy, Mr Burke; you do have the job."

He brought me into the assembly room. It was an empty auditorium with a stage at the far end. It was old and full of plastic chairs. There was a projector and large screen taking up the centre front of the room. The light was on and it was ready to go. Mr McPhillips had to go to take a phone call and asked me if I needed anything. Well, where would I begin? I told him I was fine. I had no idea where I was to stand, what I should say, or who was going to want to listen to me. It was a frightening experience. I felt alone and vulnerable in the auditorium. Outside I could hear hearty laughter, shouts and banter.

I got to the top of the hall, pulled a small table over from the wall and placed it in front of the chairs. I put down a few little plastic cards with the names of drugs on them. I took the little case I had and set it on the table. I opened it; inside there were some examples of drugs. (Only imitation drugs, not the real thing!) Then I set down five sheets of paper – the actual legal documents showing my convictions. I looked at those three items – one to show them what it looks like, one to tell them what it was like and one to educate them on what it could be like. I switched off the overhead projector and I looked down at the little table in front of me. "God, you sure have a sense of humour," I said. "A one-man multi-media event."

I heard the footsteps and the muffled restrained chatter as a group of about 200 young people were escorted in. They were all going to go to university within a few months, and they had a confidence about their life. I was looking down at the conviction sheet: fourteen for drugs offences, seventeen for forgery, eight for theft – the list went on. I took a deep breath. "Good morning, gentlemen," I began, and took it from there.

The moment I lifted the police record and said, "Here are my qualification certificates that allow me to talk about drugs", the Lord had them captured. I then did a little card game on the dangers of drugs – the misconceptions of what is dangerous or falsely "not so dangerous". With each statistic, and a bit of humour, I unravelled my real life story. The names, the places and the memories came flooding out. I was amazed to see the students listening intently and taking it all in.

As I walked out of that school that day, if someone had told me the number of students I would eventually talk to – not only to speak to them and teach them, but to share with them and learn from them – I would not have believed it. From there I moved into school after school. The phone didn't stop. I reached a target of 10,000 young people in that first year.

There is a question-and-answer session after my life story. Some questions are about drugs, but the majority are along the lines of, *What do you mean when you say you met Jesus?* And that sums it up – there is a hunger out there. We have got to learn to feed it.

From working in schools and colleges I have come to realise what is going on out there in the streets. I learned what matters to young people today. And it is not rocket science. It can be summed up like this: they don't care what you know until they know you care. Young people are as hungry for love as we all are. A lot of them have turned to drink and drugs as a result of losing the love of a father or mother, or because of family break-up. Our young people are lost today because they no longer have the same respect for Church and State; but they do have a respect for people who can turn around and say: *I'm not here to preach at you or to lecture you. I am here to share that I care about you, and I care that you don't go down the road I went down. But as much as I care about you, I have to tell you that there is one who cares about you more* – and I point the way to a relationship with Christ. Parents, teachers, lecturers, professors, psychiatrists, psychologists and all would be amazed if they sat in one of those sessions because they would see with their own eyes and feel with their own heart the real hunger that the young people have for a relationship with God, which would take away the emptiness that haunts them, instead of trying to drown it with alcohol or burying it with pills or covering it up with powder.

The emptiness is not something that everyone is aware of. It is just inside us – that timidity, that brevity of life. I think it has been put there deliberately by God so that we can look for him. Because if we didn't feel those feelings we would be so cocky and self-assured that we would waltz merrily on our way to death and never think about what would happen afterwards. The only ones who don't seem to feel it are the high achievers – the ones going around with the folders under their arms; the parents, too caught up in their own lives; everyone going around and around like little mice in the wheels. They are going so fast they are not thinking. And they are doing it for the same reason, avoiding the question: *Is that all there is?* But if you could just grab the wheel and say, *Hold on! Stop!*, then I wonder what would happen?

Young people are up to their eyeballs with religion, but they are not fed up with relationships. My programme involves getting young people to laugh at their own ideas about "safe" drugs, like tobacco, alcohol or cannabis, and to realise the dangers and face them. But it is the life story I tell, the centrepiece, that hopefully changes their hearts and minds, not only about drugs, but about God.

If I needed any convincing that my testimony was helping others, I needn't have looked further than the students. Their reactions are always positive. There are many examples I could give to show how God uses this work; here is just one.

Two years ago I was contacted by the Head of a College for Further Education, who wanted me to speak to a group of students who, for various reasons, had left

High School at an early age. They were returning to education at the college. The Head told me I was being asked to give the talk there because four years earlier in a High School in Belfast I had told my life story. In that earlier audience was a fourteen-year-old girl, pregnant and up to her eyes on drugs. This girl told the Head that my talk had changed her life. She had given up drugs and became a good mother. She was now sitting her GCSE exams with the college, and she was waiting outside to meet me. I met Rose outside the college and we talked. What an absolute privilege it is to do this work.

I firmly believe, having seen all I have in my lifetime, and having done all I did, that anyone can change, if they let God into their hearts.

I always used to mention Emma in my testimony in the schools. I would talk about her and explain how the break-up came about and what it did to us. I was giving my talk in a school in Omagh when a young girl came up to me afterwards and asked, "Do you ever see your daughter now?"

"No."

"Do you ever think about her?"

"Yes I do, every day."

As she walked away I saw tears begin to fall from that girl's eyes, and I just knew instinctively that she was really asking her own very personal question: *My dad has walked out on me. I wonder does he ever think about and care about me?*

I came home that day and I prayed earnestly to God that there would be contact between Emma and me. I didn't know how he was going to do it. I had previously sent letters to an address in London which had been returned: *Not known at this address*. So I had no idea where Emma was. Yet a week later the phone rang – and it was Emma. Somehow one of my letters had scraped through. Some people might say that it was just a great coincidence, but I know it was a God-incidence.

There I was, sitting at the bottom of the stairs at home, with the receiver in my hand. I was talking to her as a married man with a young son called Matthew. I had a job that I liked and the peace of God. But when I spoke to my daughter for the first time and she said, "This is Emma, your daughter," I wept, and they were tears of joy. We chatted about everything; laughed and cried. Everything that had happened in the past seemed to melt away. Of course, I knew there were a lot of unresolved issues, but we never talked about things like that. We chatted like father and daughter.

The phone calls were followed by letters and photos. I had to reconcile myself to looking at this blonde eighteen-year-old and convincing myself that this was the same little girl whom I had watched being wheeled away from my life in her pushchair all those years ago. Emma was very enthusiastic about our new relationship and she took an interest in my new life.

At the same time, it was a big issue for Hilary. Of course, I had told her all about Emma. But we had our new son and it is not hard to imagine the trauma she went through, thinking about her husband's long-lost daughter.

Emma even talked about coming over for a visit. This was big thing for Hilary to accept, but she did accept it.

I was cautious, though, because while I wanted to meet Emma, I would rather have met her on neutral ground. However, it never really came to be an issue because, even though we had all agreed that she could come over to visit, God had other ideas. At the time we thought she would visit, she was given a holiday in Greece with her grandparents. When Emma returned from holiday, the letter-writing and the phone calls continued. The only thing I can say here is that I really messed up. I am not going to go into details, for both Emma's sake and my own, but I will say that I made a stupid mistake.

I have since tried many many times to phone and write to Emma, but all communication has been broken. I am going to use this opportunity now to say how sorry I am to Emma. I wish I could turn the clock back and wipe the slate clean, so that we could continue to get to know each other. So Emma, if you are reading this, please phone or write to me. I hope and pray that you will.

I am sure Emma lives her own life now, but I hope she knows that she is always in my heart and always welcome in my home. I do hope to meet her one day. I had grieved for her for years until she came back into my life and I was reunited with her. I thank God for giving me that.

Chapter 34

I had one outstanding offence – trying to pass a forged script. It had happened just weeks before I became a Christian. About seven months into my "new life", I came up before Lisburn Magistrates' Court. I went into court armed with several letters from Christian organisations and churches outlining how there had been a "change" in my life. I handed them over to the Magistrate. He looked at them and said: "Drugs . . . Where is this man's prescription? How many did he write for?" The police thought it was just going to be a walk-over for me, so they didn't actually bring the prescription. The Magistrate said to them: "Go up and get that prescription and bring it down to me. Remand him in the cells." So I sat in the cells thinking: *Lord, here am I coming to court as a Christian, telling him I am a Christian now and that this is the last time they will ever see me in their courts. If I had said I am a poor drug addict, poor me – I would have walked out by now.*

The prescription was brought to the court and I was brought up from the cell. The Magistrate read a letter from the church and then he said, "It says here you are a Christian. But I've seen these letters before from people. I haven't a lot of time for any of this nonsense. It would be in my mind to put you in prison. However, I'll remand the case for three months, and when you come back, we will see if you really are a Christian." That week the local paper reported it under the headline, "Man Receives Three Months' Grace". How apt!

I came back to the court three months later. My Probation Officer stood up, saying: "I have never seen such a change in anyone in all my time." The letters were flowing up to the Magistrate from different Christian organisations. The Magistrate looked at them all and said, "Well, I still have my doubts. But your Probation Officer has recommended you get just six months' probation." He continued, "I would rather put you in prison but I will give you eighteen months' probation, not six. If I see you in my court again, be sure, Mr Burke, that you will go to prison for a very long time." I walked out of that court thinking: *Lord, what was that all about?*

Two years later, I was driving down the motorway. I switched on the radio and as the beat got louder, my foot went down on the accelerator. There was a police car just up ahead and I was waved in and charged with speeding.

A couple of months later, I had to go to Banbridge Magistrates' Court. I went in with my brother Raymond. I was expecting to get a hefty fine, maybe a couple of points onto my licence. But in I walked . . . and guess who was up on the bench? The same Magistrate. He looked at me and I looked at him, and there was a spark of recognition. I leaned over to my brother and said, "I am in deep trouble here. This guy hates me." I saw other people there, professional people who had never done anything wrong in their lives before, who were getting £400 fines, points on their licences, being disqualified.

I stood up in the dock. I didn't even have a solicitor with me. The Magistrate asked me, "What have you got to say for yourself?"

"Well, nothing. I'm sorry, I just put the foot down on the accelerator; I didn't really realise I was doing that speed."

"It says here, you are a counsellor. What council do you work for?"

"I am not that kind of counsellor. I work with addicts as well as going into schools."

And the penny truly dropped; I could see in his eyes that he remembered me.

He said, "So you would need your car for this kind of work?"

"I would."

"What kind of counselling do you do?"

"Christian counselling."

"I'll tell you what I am going to do," he said. "I am going to give you the lowest fine possible by law, which is forty pounds, and no points will be put onto your licence."

Imagine: two years had passed by and I knew God had used that event to speak to that young Magistrate, to let him know that, yes, sometimes people do come before you and that God has changed their lives.

Chapter 35

People often ask me if I feel sorry for the things I've done. Of course I do. I have cried buckets, rivers and oceans of tears over some of the things I have done. I've been so remorseful on occasions that I could not even lift my head, it was so heavy with shame. But I was never repentant until that day in 1994. From that point, though, I was not just sorry for what I had done; I was turning my back on it and allowing Christ to take the reins of my life for good. The difference now is that my ultimate goal in life is to be made more like Him; and the more I am, the happier I become.

There is nothing behind a bar that could tempt me in a million years. There is not a dealer who could offer me a million pounds worth of cocaine and say, *You can take it, God will not mind.* I still wouldn't take it. That is the strength and freedom I have found and it is only found through Christ. I did not find it in rehab. I had been there and I knew what they had to offer. What they offer is a battle and I respect those that take on that battle. But personally I could not battle. I could not be writing this today, except by the grace of God, His strength and His Holy Spirit.

God is not some anonymous spirit, or a "concept". He is not a quick fix, or an emotional high that fizzles out a week later. The reality is Jesus Himself, and only Him. Christ made it possible for all of us to know him in a personal way. Our part is simply to reach out in faith asking him to take our hand.

When I visit parents who have problems with their children, I don't just say, "Pray for them," though I do believe that is the most important thing. I also say "Be open for them" – do what my parents did for me. My parents stood at the end of the street of drink and drugs and prayed the whole time. But they were always within sight, no matter how far down that road I got. My father told me one time, "Jackie, always remember this: even if you were to go over the water and commit murder, there will always be a home for you here, and I will always love you. You will still be my son." And those words also saved my life.

Prayer is so vital. People whom I had never set eyes on, whom I never knew but who knew about me, and some Christians who saw me in the street during my worst times; they all prayed for me. I just feel that we need to pray and to believe. We need to pray for the protection of our kids. I pray for my children, that, if they ever go down that road, God will be keeping His protective hand on them while they find out that there is no real answer to that emptiness inside, that nothing can fill it except for God.

After I became a Christian, I prayed that my mother would see five years of my new life, but as I write she has seen thirteen. My mother's birthday is the 30th of August and I remember thinking in 1995 that she was celebrating her first birthday with me as a Christian. What a birthday it was! I tried to give her something, but she said, "Don't worry, you gave me the greatest gift. The greatest birthday present I've ever had."

Somebody asked me once how I knew it was Jesus Christ who had saved me that day. I can't explain it. I just had the knowledge that, despite all I'd been through, the answer was there, right in front of me, all along.

From an early age, I thought there had to be more to life. But the hippy era and the drugs were like a false dawn. I was sure I could take God on my own terms; I could do what I wanted to do and still have God in my back pocket if I needed Him. But God does not work that way. I had to find out the hard way and I thank Him that He gave me the grace to come back.

If somebody said to me that I just swapped my addiction to drugs for an addiction to Jesus, I would say: "Well, the drugs could never give me what He gives me. Is there any wonder I am addicted to Him?" I know I am addicted to Jesus because I will take any opening or opportunity to tell people about the Good News. No one can ever say I pushed it on them; it is only when they ask or when God provides an opportunity. So I have no problem being called a Jesus addict, because I am. I just wish I was addicted more. I wish I had more Christ in my life.

I am also often asked if I would have the faith I now have if I hadn't gone through everything I went through. The answer to that is, I don't know. But if I'm being asked if I have any regrets, then I do have one major regret: that I didn't keep that commitment I made at fourteen, because I could have been living the life I have now throughout my whole life. I have met people in my life who have never touched a drink, never took drugs, who became Christians at a young age and who lived their life like that. They are very happy people.

If I had remained a Christian, living that journey from the age of fourteen, my brother might not have died, and if he did, I wouldn't have poured the drink. Emma might not have been left behind. She might not even have been conceived by me. But only God knows who is right. I am the most grateful man on earth, because I have had thirteen years that nobody would have thought possible. Those who knew me in Lisburn may ask, "Whatever happened to Jackie Burke?" If you were to ask them if they ever thought they would see me as I am now, the answer for most of them would be "No." As God raised me from the dead, I thank Him for it.

So God has set me free. Why? Because he loved me. All through those years he was there. It is the same love he has for me today. I find this unconditional love amazing. If you are reading this book and if you are an addict, I want to pass on to you the gift of life that was given to me. I suppose it is very like the old saying – *"One beggar showing another beggar where to find some bread".*

As a drug addict I was willing to try anything, follow anyone, if it meant I could get off the drugs. But of course I knew part of that was an addiction in itself – rehab, new friends, new experiences. As an addict I would have tried anything as long as I had control over it. No addict wants to hear about this "God stuff" if they have to let go, have no control.

I could say you need to lie down on a bed of nails twice a week, or you need to hug a tree, and at the end of the week you will find the peace you are searching for. All rubbish! But an addict might rather do that than surrender to the Lord. The only answer to addiction, the only freedom from its entrapment, is Christ.

You are probably saying: "I am not into all that 'God stuff'." Whenever I get that reaction from the students, I tell them to go home, find a quiet place and pray: *"Lord I am not really sure if you are there, but with the little bit of faith that I do have, I just ask you, if you are real, then reveal yourself to me, in Jesus' name. Amen."*

Some of you may have relatives and friends caught up in the vice of drink and drugs. You are at a loss about what to do. While every situation is different, and you cannot condense all addicts into one convenient box, some things are similar to all. I was well versed at lying, cheating and a master at the "poor me". Addicts are supreme at manipulation and build up their own brownie points in order to knock them down in a well-planned drink and drugs bender. That is not to say addicts are "bad" people or uncaring. I have never met an addict yet who didn't have a good heart. But these traits are all part of addiction, and are sometimes unintentionally reinforced by those who love them. Addicts feed them lines like: *"I'm not well. I'm ill. I have a disease. I can't help myself . . ."* While there is an element of truth to some of these, there is also deception.

So to those looking on – show your love by keeping the door of your heart open, despite the many times they may break it. But at the same time, learn to close it for your own protection when you need to.

People do not change until they realise that there are consequences to their actions. It is a fine line that every family member and friend has to walk. You love them, you want them to change, and just when you are getting through, they blow it apart. At times like that, don't give up – look up! I did not find "religion". I found a relationship. When people ask me to define what religion I follow, I say I am a "spiritual gypsy and a traveller with Christ". He has given me hope and I pray you find the same. You have seen through my life story how low I became, yet through prayer, love and the hope of Christ, I was changed. If it can happen for me, it can happen for anyone.

My God is a God of second chances. There are thousands of second chances I could tell you about from the night that changed my life, to this day. My mother is in her eighties. Every day we talk together on the phone. Yesterday was no different. At the end of the conversation, the one question she always asks is, "Jackie, where are you going tomorrow, son?" In other words, which school or college would I be visiting? So I tell her, so that she can pray.

Only right now she is not praying for me; she's praying for all those affected by drugs. She's praying that my experience will not just go into your head and that you will forget it five minutes later, but rather that it will go in and remain in your heart.

One day I had to go out to pick up a prescription for Hilary, who had been sick with the 'flu. Matthew and Rachel wanted to come along and I said OK. It was a windy, rainy day. We parked the car. We crossed the road and headed towards the chemist – the same one I used to stand outside at eight o'clock every morning, the same one where I got my daily supply of drugs, the same one I couldn't bear to be away from. And as I watched Matthew and Rachel do their little dance through the puddles and the rain, laughing to themselves, I caught a glimpse of myself in the moment, for one brief second. I saw myself lying in those puddles or waiting at the door of the chemist begging for a few pills so that I could face another day. And at that very moment, both of my kids looked back and shouted, "Come on, Dad, take our hands". This was my new life, my life, my second chance at happiness and love, and I reached out and grasped it with both hands.

Direct to your home!

If you enjoyed this book why not visit our website:

www.poolbeg.com

and get another book delivered straight to your home or to a friend's home!

www.poolbeg.com

All orders are despatched within 24 hours.